THE AENEID OF VIRGIL
A COMMENTARY

Current titles in this series:

THE AENEID OF VIRGIL

A Commentary based on the
Translation of C. Day Lewis,
with Introduction and Glossary

R.D. Williams

Published by Bristol Classical Press
General Editor: John H. Betts

This impression 2004
First edition published in 1985, with assistance from
the Society for the Promotion of Roman Studies, by
Bristol Classical Press
an imprint of
Gerald Duckworth & Co. Ltd.
90-93 Cowcross Street, London EC1M 6BF
Tel: 020 7490 7300
Fax: 020 7490 0080
inquiries@duckworth-publishers.co.uk
www.ducknet.co.uk

A catalogue record for this book is available
from the British Library

ISBN 0 86292 044 2

Cover illustration: the fleet
of Aeneas, after a fourth-century AD
Romano-British mosaic from Low Ham Villa,
Somerset; in the Castle Museum, Taunton.
(For a full discussion see J.M.C. Toynbee,
Art in Roman Britain [1962]
203-5, no. 200, pl. 235.)
[Drawing by Patrick Harrison]

Printed and bound in Great Britain by
Antony Rowe Ltd, Eastbourne

Contents

Preface

This commentary on Day Lewis's translation of Virgil's *Aeneid* is intended to supply explanations of fact and aids towards appreciation for students of Virgil who cannot read the *Aeneid* in Latin. The sweep and impetus of Day Lewis's poetry conveys to the twentieth-century reader of Virgil a great deal of the essence of the *Aeneid*; but necessarily there often occur references which the less experienced reader will not understand, and also explanation is called for where the translation does not fully represent the Latin nuance (as is bound to happen in any translation), and where the poetic impact of particular passages may not be fully appreciated. In addition I have tried to elucidate the use by Virgil of certain value words which play a great part in the themes of the poem, words such as *pietas* and *furor*.

I have prefaced the commentary on each book with a brief survey of the book's subject-matter and its treatment; this supplements the general discussion of the *Aeneid's* literary qualities, which I have given in the Introduction, by referring to the main points again in their context. I have added a glossary which explains all proper names except those of persons and places which occur once or twice only and are of no special significance. In the four appendices I have given samples of a fuller type of literary appreciation.

I wish to express my thanks to the Society for the Promotion of Roman Studies for a generous grant towards the publication of this commentary; to the Hogarth Press for permission to use Day Lewis's translation; and to the Bristol Classical Press for all their help and encouragement in the preparation of the book.

R.D. Williams
Reading, 1985

vii

Introduction

The *Aeneid* of Virgil has been more widely read and studied[1] than any other Latin poem; its popularity in Roman and in Medieval times is reflected in the excellence and antiquity of the manuscripts which we possess, giving us far better evidence for the text than is the case with any other classical author. It has been admired for widely diverse reasons: in Roman times it was regarded as the supreme patriotic expression of the nation's greatness; in Medieval times the emphasis was often on the Christian values in the poem (frequently allegorically interpreted), so that for Dante Virgil was the great master and guide; in the Renaissance and afterwards Virgil's perfection of form and narrative technique served as a model for writers like Spenser and Milton; in the nineteenth century critics appreciated especially the pathos and the sadness expressed in Virgil's 'accents of brooding sorrow'. In the twentieth century we can see how all these angles of approach are legitimate, and how the poem is in fact a synthesis of different aspects of the human and the divine world, juxtaposed and presented in varied poetic situations. The poem is not merely Roman (though it is that); it is universal and timeless in its exploration of the permanent problems of human experience.

1   VIRGIL'S LIFE AND WORKS   70 – 19 BCE

Publius Vergilius Maro was born in northern Italy near Mantua in 70 B.C. He was brought up on his father's farm and

---

1   For the influence of Virgil see especially D. Comparetti, *Vergil in the Middle Ages*, trans. Benecke, 1895; D. P. Harding, *The Club of Hercules*, Urbana, 1962 (about Virgil and Milton); and my chapter in D. R. Dudley's *Virgil (Studies in Latin Literature and its Influence)*, London, 1969, pp. 119ff. (with bibliography given there).

1

was always deeply in love with the Italian countryside. Subsequently he moved to Rome, and then to Naples. Early on he became accepted in the literary court circle under the patronage of Maecenas, and got to know the leading figures in Roman political and military life, including the future Emperor Augustus. He played no part in political or military activities himself, but he was closely in touch with those who did. He lived most of his life during a period of disastrous civil wars which caused havoc to Italian farming, and like many of his contemporaries he felt a profound relief when Augustus' victory at Actium in 31 B.C. seemed to mark the beginning of a stable period of peace.

Virgil's earliest certain work[2] comprises a collection of ten poems called *Eclogues* or *Bucolics*, composed between perhaps 42 and 37 B.C. These are pastoral poems largely based on the Greek writer Theocritus but containing certain innovations, such as the idyllic and imaginary setting in Arcadia and the inclusion in this setting among the shepherds of real figures from the contemporary world, like Gallus and Varus and Pollio. The most famous of these poems, the fourth, prophesies the birth of a child who will introduce a new Golden Age; it was for long regarded as a prophecy of Christ and known as the Messianic Eclogue.

Next Virgil wrote the *Georgics* (37–30 B.C.), a didactic poem on agriculture in four books, the first concerned with the growing of crops, the second with trees, the third with cattle and the fourth with bees. The poem ends with a mythological tale about Aristaeus and his bees, including within it the story of Orpheus and Eurydice; here we see the poet writing narrative in a supernatural setting of the kind he was to use extensively in the *Aeneid*. The *Georgics* reflects Virgil's love of the countryside and his pride in Italy – it is designed not so much to instruct as to inspire his fellow-countrymen with something

---

2 There exist a number of poems attributed at various times to Virgil, and collectively referred to as the Virgilian Appendix. Very few of these are likely to have been written by Virgil.

of his own love of Nature seen as part of the total divine cosmos in which we live.

Finally, Virgil turned to the epic poem for which he had long been preparing himself, and occupied the rest of his life (30–19 B.C.) on the *Aeneid*. The poem is based on two deep desires, one to emulate and to some extent reproduce in a Roman setting the epic poetry of Homer which had cast such a spell over him; and the second to express the achievements and ideals and hopes of Rome, as she recovered from the civil wars and sought to establish peace for herself and the whole world. In 19 B.C. Virgil set out on a voyage to Greece, perhaps to acquire local colour for the final revision of his poem, but fell ill of fever and died on his return to Italy. His last request was that the *Aeneid* should be burnt, but Augustus countermanded this, and the poem was published posthumously. It lacks the final detailed touches of revision, but in all major respects it is complete.

2   SUMMARY OF THE *AENEID*

The poem tells the story of how the Trojan prince Aeneas had it laid upon him as a divine mission that he should escape from the burning ruins of Troy and lead a band of exiles to found a new city in the West, which was destined to become ruler and civiliser of the whole world.

Book 1   The narrative begins when the Trojans, after seven years of wanderings, are just off the coast of Sicily, and at last very near their goal. But Juno arouses a storm which drives them off course to the coast of Africa. Here Venus in disguise meets Aeneas and directs him to Dido's city of Carthage. The Trojans are hospitably received, and through Venus' schemes Dido falls in love with Aeneas. A banquet is held, and Dido asks Aeneas to tell the story of his wanderings.

Book 2   Aeneas tells the story of Troy's last night. Through the trickery of Sinon the wooden horse is taken into the city and the Greeks hidden in it emerge and open the gates to their comrades. Aeneas sees a vision of Hector's ghost telling him to

3

escape and found a new city elsewhere. The fighting culminates in the slaughter of the old King Priam. Aeneas, prompted by Venus, collects his family and escapes with his father Anchises and his little son Ascanius (Iulus), but his wife Creusa is lost in the confusion. Her ghost appears to Aeneas and reiterates Hector's message.

Book 3 The wanderings This book contains the long story of Aeneas' seven-year wanderings as he tries to find the destined site for his new city. The Trojans go to Thrace, to Delos, to Crete; then past the islands of the Harpies and past Actium to Buthrotum where Helenus delivers a long prophecy. They then get their first sight of Italy, land near Etna and encounter the Cyclops and finally sail round Sicily to its north-western corner. Anchises, who has played a large part in this book encouraging and advising his son, dies at Libybaeum, and Aeneas has now brought the story up to the point at which the narrative began in Book 1.

Book 4 Dido and Aeneas The narrative resumes after Aeneas' speech, and describes the passionate love of Dido for Aeneas. But Aeneas is warned by a message from heaven that he must leave Carthage in order to found his new city. He immediately accepts that he must put his divine duty above his personal inclinations, and after he has vainly tried to explain his reasons to Dido, he and the Trojans depart. Dido in frenzy and despair kills herself.

Book 5 Sicily and the funeral of Anchises The Trojans revisit Sicily and celebrate funeral observances and games at the tomb of Anchises. Inspired by Juno, the Trojan women set fire to their ships, but Jupiter saves all except four. Some Trojans are left behind, and the remainder sail on to Italy. On the very last stage of the journey the faithful helmsman Palinurus is lost overboard.

Book 6 Aeneas in the underworld. Aeneas visits the temple of Apollo at Cumae in order to go down to the underworld to learn more fully of his future destiny from the ghost of his father Anchises. Accompanied by the Sibyl he descends and first encounters the ghosts of his past, Palinurus, Dido and Deiphobus, before meeting his father in Elysium. Anchises shows him a pageant of Roman heroes waiting to be born if Aeneas fulfils his mission. Aeneas returns to earth heartened and resolute.

4

✓ 2/08/09

✓ leave for now go to p. 6

Book 7   The Trojans reach the mouth of the Tiber and are well received by King Latinus who betroths his daughter Lavinia to Aeneas. But Juno intervenes and arouses violent opposition in Queen Amata and Turnus, Lavinia's suitor. War breaks out, and the book ends with a catalogue of the Italian forces.

Aeneas seeks the help of Evander, Venus commissions his shield.

Book 8   Aeneas leaves the Trojan camp to seek help from Evander, an Arcadian settled on the future site of Rome. Evander promises a contingent of troops led by his son Pallas. Meanwhile Venus has new armour made for Aeneas: at the end of the book the pictures on the shield, a series of scenes from future Roman history, are described.

Book 9   In the absence of Aeneas Turnus attacks the Trojan camp. Nisus and Euryalus make a night sally to try to establish contact with Aeneas, but are both killed. Turnus achieves great deeds on the battlefield and breaks into the Trojan camp, but made reckless by success fails to open the gates to let his army in, and is himself finally forced to escape.

Book 10   Aeneas returns with Pallas and full-scale battle continues. Pallas is confronted by Turnus and brutally killed: Turnus strips him of his armour. Aeneas in mad anger rages over the battlefield, killing many of the enemy including the young Lausus and his father Mezentius.

Book 11   The Trojans hold funeral rites for Pallas: the news of his death reaches Evander, who prays for vengeance on Turnus. In the subsequent battle scenes the great deeds and death of the warrior-maiden Camilla are described.

Book 12   A truce is organised so that single combat between Aeneas and Turnus can decide the war, but it is broken and full-scale fighting develops again. Following the siege of Latinus' capital and the suicide of Queen Amata Turnus realises that he must confront Aeneas. The scene moves to Olympus, where Juno is reconciled with the Trojans on condition that the Italians shall be the dominant partners in the alliance from which will spring the Roman people. In the final scene on earth Aeneas wounds Turnus, and when Turnus begs for mercy he sees the captured insignia of young Pallas on Turnus' shoulder and in hot anger kills him.

Thus at the end of the poem the way is clear for Aeneas to found his city. The subsequent events which lead to the eventual foundation of Rome nearly four hundred years later had been prophesied by Jupiter in his speech in Book 1 (257 ff.). Upon Aeneas' death his son Ascanius would take over the rule of the settlement at Lavinium, and then transfer the seat of power to Alba Longa. Here a series of kings would rule for three hundred years until Romulus, son of Mars and the priestess Rhea Silvia, would found the city of Rome. To these Romans, Jupiter said,

> ... I set no bounds, either in space or time;
> Unlimited power I give them. (1.278–9)

3 THE SOURCES OF THE *AENEID*

The legend of Aeneas The story of how the Trojan prince Aeneas left burning Troy in search of a new home in the West was already several centuries old by Virgil's time,[3] and it had become especially well-known from the time when the Romans came into close contact with the Greeks in the third century B.C. But the legend had the enormous advantage for Virgil of being fluid and flexible, so that it could be reshaped according to his special poetic purposes. In particular the story of Dido was very largely Virgil's original creation: there is some evidence that she was mentioned in Naevius (*c.* 220 B.C.), but she did not figure at all in the prose versions of the legend (as we can read them in Livy and Dionysius of Halicarnassus), and the great concentration in Virgil's version on her love for Aeneas was undoubtedly something quite new. Again, Virgil has changed the normal account of the death of Anchises so

---

3 For a fuller account of the legend (with bibliography) see my edition of *Aeneid* 3, Intro. pp. 7 ff., and G. K. Galinsky, *Aeneas, Sicily and Rome*, Princeton, 1969.

that he could motivate the second visit to Sicily and the funeral celebrations (Book 5); he has greatly altered the traditional account of the wars in Italy; and he has used all kinds of devices (prophecies, visions, descriptions of pictures) in order to link the distant past with the present, so that his story is not merely one of antiquarian interest but also an exposition of the ideals and problems of Augustan Rome.

① Homer

Literary sources   Far and away the most important literary source of the *Aeneid* is the poetry of Homer. Virgil has not only employed Homeric epic techniques and machinery (like similes, divine action, catalogue of forces) and whole episodes (descent to the underworld, funeral games, storm and shipwreck) and frequent verbal reminiscences, but also has used the Homeric heroic age as the setting for his own narrative. Thus he could continue and conclude the famous Trojan story from a Roman point of view, and he could show Aeneas as the heroic warrior who had to step out of the heroic world into a proto-Roman world. This relationship with Homer gave the opportunity of putting Homeric values side by side with Roman values, of weighing the nature and validity of Aeneas' more social virtues with the direct and impetuous individualism of the heroes of the *Iliad* and the *Odyssey*. More is said on this subject under the heading *The major themes of the poem* (section 6, below).

② Greek tragedy

Greek tragedy contributed to Virgil's poem; in some senses Dido's story is a tragedy complete in itself, and so is the story of Turnus. The later Greek writer Apollonius of Rhodes, who wrote of the Argonauts and the love of Jason and Medea, provided a source for some features of the love of Dido and Aeneas.

③ Roman writers

Among Roman writers Virgil certainly used the patriotic epic of Ennius (now surviving only in fragments), often imitating the phraseology and diction; in passages of pathos (like the death of Euryalus, the funeral of Pallas and especially the story of Dido) he turned to Catullus, particularly his sixty-fourth poem which contains an account of Theseus' desertion of Ariadne.

It will be seen (and it is most important to stress this) that Virgil has used the rich literary heritage of Greek and Latin literature to enrich his presentation of the story of Aeneas. It was traditional with the Romans to use the work of their literary predecessors in their own work; originality for its own sake was not sought after, least of all in epic. But when this has been said, it must be emphasised that Virgil has always adapted this material, used it for his own special purposes, produced in fact a synthesis of the themes and moods of earlier poets within the large-scale framework of his epic poem. We see the heroic bravery, the rash impulses of the Homeric warrior set against the specially Roman qualities of family life, social virtues, deep religious piety; we see the stern note of patriotism which filled Ennius' poem set against the pathos, the sorrow of the lonely individual, which Catullus so often expressed. The essence of the *Aeneid* is the interplay of opposing attitudes to life's deepest problems, taken from past literature or from Virgil's own experience of life, and presented in a whole series of poetically organised episodes throughout the poem.

4 THE PATRIOTIC ASPECTS OF THE AENEID

There were, as we have seen, two driving forces that led Virgil to devote his life to preparing for and writing his epic poem. The first was the spell which Homer's poetry had cast over him and his desire to be the Roman Homer; and the second was his feeling of patriotic optimism as the civil wars came to an end and Rome under Augustus could look forward to a time of peace and prosperity, a new Golden Age. These were hopes which Virgil had in common with many Romans at the beginning of Augustus' reign; it was a period when national confidence was at last restored after the horrors of the last decades of the Republic, and this sense of excitement and success is reflected in the *Aeneid*.

The main way in which Virgil expresses his patriotic optimism is by way of dreams and visions, and by prophetic descriptions. Many times (especially in Book 3) Aeneas receives heartening prophecies that he will found a people which one day will rule

8

the world; three passages in particular give sustained prophe-
cies of the greatness of Rome. The first of these comes early in
the poem (1.257ff.) when Jupiter prophesies to his daughter
Venus that the Romans will conquer and civilise the world,
and introduce an era of settled prosperity and peace ('Then
shall the age of violence be mellowing into peace', 291). This
passage is fully analysed in Appendix 1. The second great
patriotic exposition is at the end of Book 6, when Aeneas in the
underworld is shown the ghosts of great Roman heroes of
future history waiting to be born. The passage begins with a
pageant of ancient Alban kings, then concentrates on Romu-
lus the founder of Rome and then on Augustus, the second
founder ('And here, here is the man, the promised one you
know of– Caesar Augustus, son of a god, destined to rule where
Saturn ruled of old in Latium, and there bring back the age of
gold', 6.791–4). There follows a long line of Roman kings and
heroes of the Republic (Brutus, Camillus, the Gracchi, the
Scipios and many more), and the passage ends with the
famous summary of Rome's mission ('But, Romans, never
forget that government is your medium! Be this your art:–
to practise men in the habit of peace, generosity to the con-
quered, and firmness against aggressors). See also the note
on 6.756–853.

The third passage is at the end of Book 8 (626ff.): Virgil
describes the pictures of future Roman history which the god
Vulcan had engraved on the new shield which he made for
Aeneas. Many of the famous scenes from Roman history are
depicted around the edge, and in the centre are pictures of the
battle of Actium, showing the victory of Augustus over Antony
and Cleopatra which inaugurated the Roman empire and
seemed to promise the restoration of that peace and stability
which Jupiter had promised at the end of his speech in Book 1.
This passage is more fully analysed in the note on 8.626ff. p 89.

Two other methods by which Virgil reflects his patriotic pride
may be briefly mentioned. First he employs what is called
aetiological association, that is to say the association of the
present with the past by reference to the origins of con-
temporary institutions or buildings or topography. Sometimes

* (the history of present customs &
names of places
present festivals

9

he does this by name association (Iulus as the ancestor of the Julians, Palinurus giving his name to Cape Palinurus and so on); sometimes by promise of future events (Aeneas vows a great temple to Apollo and a cult for the Sibyl); sometimes obliquely (the rites at Anchises' tomb clearly suggesting the Roman Parentalia; the ceremonies for Hercules in Book 8 indicating the development of the annual celebrations in his honour in the Rome of Virgil's day); sometimes directly, as when he says that the Trojan Game, first celebrated at Anchises' tomb (5.553 ff.), was handed on to Alba and thence to Rome (5.600 ff.).

Finally a method which Virgil uses to link the Trojan past with the Roman present is by means of character portrayal. Aeneas is in the story a Trojan, but he is learning to be a Roman. His attitude towards the gods and his constant observation of religious rites and worship are those of Virgil's own time. Above all his quality of dutifulness, of the acceptance of social and family and religious responsibilities is one on which the Romans especially prided themselves: it is reflected in Aeneas' constant epithet *pius* (see note on 1.10) and in his endeavours throughout the poem to sacrifice his personal inclinations to his responsibilities towards his people and his gods.

5   RELIGION IN THE *AENEID*

Above all else the *Aeneid* is a religious poem. It is based on the unquestioned belief that there exist powers outside the mortal world, that humans are not alone in the universe. This is indicated by the dominant part played in the poem by the concept of fate or destiny. The word occurs in the second line of the poem, and throughout it is clear that Aeneas' actions are guided by the fact that he has accepted the call of destiny to found his city. Constantly he worships the gods, prays to them, accepts their messages. The Olympian hierarchy plays a dominant part in the poem (as was the case in Homer): Virgil has modified the Homeric conception of the gods so as to give them added dignity, but he has accepted the idea of a double action to the plot – on one level determined, or at all events very

10

strongly influenced, by the gods, and on another level played out by the human characters.

Jupiter as king of the gods is the agent of destiny, serenely ruling over the lesser deities who have their own special functions (Neptune as god of the sea, Vulcan as god of fire and so on) and in some cases scheme against each other to defend their favourites. Venus, as mother of Aeneas, is the protective deity of the Roman mission; against her is ranged the queen of heaven, Juno, who is implacably hostile to the Trojans. Much of the suffering in the poem is the direct result of Juno's intervention, and yet in the end, when she is reconciled to Jupiter's insistence that she should delay the fates no longer, she asks for and gets conditions on behalf of her Italians which in fact ensure the greatness of Rome. The Roman empire, after all, was far more Italian than Trojan, and this is Juno's doing.

Virgil's gods very seeable but...

The gods are portrayed essentially in a mythological and visual way: Virgil delighted in the verbal painting of scenes which the human eye cannot see, and his Olympians are magnificently pictorial. Think of Juno striding majestically through the halls of heaven; of Neptune in his chariot, surrounded by his strange sea-deities, driving over the waves and calming the storm; of Iris descending to earth by way of her own brilliantly-coloured rainbow; of Mercury swooping down over the cliffs of Carthage like a sea-bird. This pictorial aspect of other-worldly visions was a mainspring of Virgil's poetic inspiration, and should not be underestimated when we consider why his poem contains Olympian deities. But it is of course also true that they symbolise aspects of human experience. I take two examples. The interventions of Juno ①
symbolise that aspect of human experience which seems so inexplicable in a world governed by divine providence, the sudden disaster, the unexpected and undeserved blow, the 'slings and arrows of outrageous fortune'. The apparition of ② Mercury, sent by Jupiter to Aeneas in Book 4 (265ff.), may be seen on the pictorial level on which Virgil has presented it, or it may be rationalised into what we might call the voice of God speaking to a man whose actions have been wrong in order to

also direct intervention in human life

11

inspire him to change them. Aeneas is the kind of man who can hear the voice of God when it speaks, and he acts accordingly. We might compare the 'divine voices' of Joan of Arc or of Socrates.

3/08/09

6 THE MAJOR THEMES OF THE POEM

Contrast between Turnus & Aeneas

(great) Homeric values / Roman values (pietas)

The outstanding feature of the *Aeneid* is that it explores what we may call the tensions between opposing attitudes to life. We have seen how Homer's poems enabled Virgil to make a contrast in his poem between the values of the Homeric world (to which Aeneas belonged) and those of the Roman world (which he had to found). Thus Virgil can explore the nature of Roman values by comparison with those of the heroic age, investigating where they are the same and where different. For example, through most of the poem we feel that Aeneas is trying to modify the Homeric qualities of unthinking courage and reckless individualism in the direction of a more considered and responsible attitude to life, less immediate, less exciting but more civilised. The similarity of Turnus to the Homeric hero serves to point the contrast with Aeneas – and yet on three crucial occasions Aeneas loses (or rejects) control and behaves exactly like a Homeric hero (after Pallas' death, after his own wound, and when Turnus begs for mercy). The new way of life seems not to have left the old way completely behind - should it have done?

Secondly there is the tension between the optimistic note of patriotism and the continued existence in the world of sorrow and suffering, in spite of Rome and sometimes because of Rome. I have already discussed some patriotic passages of the poem, which are very real (though critics have sometimes overlooked their importance); we may call this aspect Virgil's public voice, and I hope I have shown that we should not doubt its genuineness. But there is also Virgil's private voice, raised to protest on behalf of the lonely individual who does not belong to the cosmic scheme of things, who is brushed aside by the massive requirement of Rome's mission. This we see illustrated in the poem by the countless deaths in battle of warriors

12

on both sides (one thinks especially of Euryalus, Pallas, Lausus), and especially in the figures of the two great opponents of the Roman mission, whose lives are taken because of that mission, Dido and Turnus. Both will be discussed more fully in the section on characters in the poem: here it will be enough to say that the sympathy which Virgil arouses for Dido is so strong as to leave the reader profoundly unhappy that the Roman mission should have caused this tragedy; while Turnus, for all his faults, is a gallant young warrior who fights for what he sees to be his rights, and in accordance with what he thinks to be his duty, and pays for it with his life. The sense of tragedy at the end of Book 4 and at the end of Book 12 is so strong that it limits and modifies our optimism about Rome's golden age; but it is not true to suggest, as some have, that it wipes out the hopeful vision.

3) Thirdly we may see a tension between the human and the divine. The poem is heavily laden with the concept of fate, but it never becomes fatalistic. In a paradoxical way the human actors are essential to the fulfilment of fate – and even more paradoxically they retain their human free-will to act with or against the fates. This was a paradox well-known to the Romans from the Stoic philosophy, which taught that God was working out human destiny in accordance with his plan, but that the difference between virtue and vice was whether a human willingly followed the divine plan, or was forced to do so against his will. Virgil's position gives more emphasis to free-will; Aeneas as man of destiny has responsibilities which he must fulfil, and is often divinely aided so that he can fulfil them, but he is free at any time to reject his divine mission and revert instead to his personal wishes. This aspect of the poem is discussed more fully in the section below on the character of Aeneas.

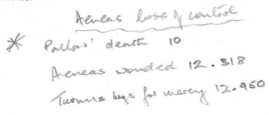

Aeneas loss of control
✳ Pallas' death 10
Aeneas wounded 12.318
Turnus begs for mercy 12.950

Aeneas

The hero of the *Aeneid* has often been criticised by people who otherwise have thought highly of the poem: Charles James Fox called him 'always either insipid or odious' and Wight Duff expressed the views of many when he said 'The *Aeneid* succeeds in spite of its hero'.[4] Generally the criticisms have suggested that he is lifeless, a kind of puppet of the gods, lacking in real human personality, a very pale shadow of Homer's Achilles.

What must be realised first and foremost is that Virgil had no intention of trying to create a new Achilles. His problem was to create a hero appropriate for an age no longer heroic. The larger-than-life impetuous splendour of an Achilles would not be appropriate for the much more complicated Roman world: the brilliant individualism of Odysseus (the most vivid individual perhaps in all literature) did not provide the kind of leadership suitable for a civilisation which placed enormous emphasis on social qualities, on responsibilities and obligations which required the individual to sacrifice his own personal desires for the good of his group, his family, his country and his gods. *Homeric individualistic hero as opposed to Roman corporate responsibility*

The new hero then must be characterised by a willingness to subordinate his own individual personality to the needs and requirements of his duty. The word which Virgil chooses for this is *pietas* ('devotion to duty') and Aeneas is called *pius* throughout the poem. When he struggles on to continue with his mission though he would much sooner not, this is due to *pietas*; when he follows the will of the gods however difficult he finds it, this is due to *pietas*; when he leaves Dido with whom he had found happiness it is because of the obligations of duty, because of *pietas*. Inevitably such a person does not cut the

---

4 For further unfavourable comments, especially during the Romantic period, see my chapter in D. R. Dudley's *Virgil (Studies in Latin Literature and its Influence)*, pp. 119ff.

figure of an Achilles, who strides confidently and magnificently through life, certain of the rightness of his actions. Aeneas is perpetually involved in uncertainties about the right course of action – he ponders, worries, lies awake at night as he tries to decide how to face each new insistent problem.

Another aspect of *pietas* is its opposition to *furor*, the irrational element in man which causes him to act on impulse rather than in accordance with reason, to lose his temper, to become wildly angry and frenzied in his behaviour, displaying the qualities of a wild animal (a lion or a tiger) rather than the rational control which is proper to man. This opposition is shown in the first simile of the poem (see note on 1.148 ff.) and the great speech of Jupiter ends on the same point (see note on 1.291 ff.). Throughout the poem Aeneas attempts by his *pietas* to overcome *furor* both in himself and in others; but his success in doing so is only intermittent, and on three notable occasions he is wholly conquered by *furor*: after Pallas' death (10.513 ff.), after his own wound (12.441 ff.), and most notably of all at the end of the poem where he yields to *furor* and kills his suppliant Turnus. *12:950*

The poem is primarily concerned with Aeneas' efforts to fulfil the divine mission laid upon him to found a new city in the West which will ultimately rule and civilise the world. We see from Books 2 and 3 how Aeneas increasingly comes to accept and understand this mission, but in the course of the poem the disasters and difficulties which come upon him are such that he frequently doubts and despairs. He has often been compared with the Christian hero who has received a divine revelation which changes his life and gives him supernatural strength to fulfil the commands of God. But this is a misleading comparison: Aeneas' acceptance of his divine mission is much weaker than that of the Christian hero. He does not draw infinite strength and determination from his mission: he sees it only dimly, with his very limited strength he struggles uncertainly towards a goal which he does not fully comprehend. *(and will never see.)*

Thus one of the dominant aspects of Aeneas' characterisation

15

is his human frailty. Throughout the first half of the poem it frequently seems that Aeneas will not be able to continue, that his resolution is insufficient to overcome all the obstacles, that the burden on his shoulders is too great for him to bear. This is made particularly clear in the first book of the poem: on Aeneas' first appearance, when his ships are beset by Juno's storm we see him frightened and in despair, all too human, in no way superhumanly resolute to overcome all trials[5]:

> At once a mortal chill went through Aeneas and
> sapped him;
> He groaned . . .

And in the speech he makes he wishes that he had died at Troy. When the storm is over he makes a heartening speech to his men, but Virgil immediately tells us that his confidence was feigned – 'his heart was sick with anxiety'.

At this point in Book 1 the scene shifts to heaven, and Jupiter tells his daughter Venus of the greatness and glory which await the Roman race once Aeneas has founded it – a series of promises which make the reader feel that whatever Aeneas has to suffer he must go on; it is essential that he should. The reader feels this because he has been privileged to see into Jupiter's book of fate; but Aeneas the mortal has not heard the speech in heaven, and must grope his way onwards on his own.

When his divine mother Venus meets him in disguise, Aeneas complains bitterly to her of the ill-fortune and calamity which has beset him: he insists that he has been following destiny's bidding, he gives himself his epithet *pius*, and yet he is now washed up on the shore of Libya, lost and almost helpless. Is this, he implies, the reward for *pietas*, the reward for sacrificing everything to a divine duty? Here he is showing not merely his human frailty in the face of overwhelming misfortune, but also

---

5   Aeneas has often been compared with a Stoic hero (see C.M. Bowra, *Greece and Rome*, 1933–4, pp. 8ff. and M.W. Edwards, *Phoenix*, 1960, pp. 151ff.) and there are indeed points of similarity. But Aeneas lacks the final rock-like endurance of the ideal Stoic, and he also lacks the Stoic ability to accept sorrow and suffering as part of the divine plan which must not be questioned.

a lack of confidence in the mission to which he has devoted himself.

This aspect of frailty and uncertainty is often again seen in the first half of the poem, especially in Book 5 after the burning of the ships, and in the first part of Book 6 when he relives his past by meeting with the ghosts of dead friends and is filled with guilt and remorse for the part which he (and his mission) had played in their deaths. It is not until the revelation made to him by Anchises of the ghosts of Roman heroes waiting to be born if he achieves his mission, that we feel at last that Aeneas will now be strong and resolute enough to continue on through all obstacles (see introductory note to Book 6). His problems in the second half of the poem are different: he is determined now to succeed, but he wants to do so with the minimum of violence. This proves to be impossible, and Aeneas now battles with the question of how to overcome violent opposition when he himself wishes the way of peace. His solution in the end is the same as the Roman solution of history – in the last resort violence must be opposed with violence. This was a solution which profoundly disturbed the peace-loving Virgil, and much of the poignancy of the second half of the poem is concerned with this tension.

Lastly something must be said of the question of human free-will. Aeneas has devoted himself to a divine mission: does this mean that he is a marionette of fate, unable to determine his own actions because they are determined for him in advance? No, it does not; not in the way Virgil has presented it in his poem. Many have felt that because the Roman mission came true it had to all the time; but this is to look at the poem back to front. We are seeing the events which led to the end-product; had the events been different the end-product would have been different. Others have argued that these things were not achieved by Aeneas but by fate and the gods who help him often in times of distress. But is there anything surprising when a man has devoted himself to a divine calling that he should receive aid and assistance from divine sources when in desperate need? Communication with the divine has become a mainspring of his actions, and this communication is likely to be at its strongest in moments of deepest crisis.

Moreover, a powerful way in which Virgil has indicated the free-will of Aeneas within this divine context is by frequently conveying through the action that Aeneas is free to give up his mission at any stage. Indeed it often seems that he is about to give up – he keeps on going by the skin of his teeth. There is one passage in the poem in which this is made absolutely explicit: when the Trojan women have burnt the ships Aeneas is in the deepest despair:

> But lord Aeneas, hard hit by this most cruel disaster,
> Was full of anxiety, and his mind kept oscillating
> Between two thoughts – should he settle down in
>   Sicily here
> And forget his destiny, or struggle on towards Italy?
>   (5.700–3)

Should he 'forget his destiny'? It was essential for the future of Rome that he should not, and although he was a frail human he did not. The Roman readers of Virgil's own time had a similar task: like Aeneas they should not forget their destiny.

✓ 3)08)09
✓ 4)08)09

Dido

The love-story of Dido and Aeneas has always been the most popular part of the *Aeneid*, and has exercised the greatest influence on subsequent literature and art. Medieval French romances used it as a favourite theme: Marlowe's *Dido, Queen of Carthage* is closely based on Virgil: the operas by Purcell and Berlioz are well-known. It has been well said that Dido is the only character created by the Romans to have found a place in world literature (all the other most famous characters of antiquity begin with the Greeks).

Virgil's presentation of the story falls into three sections. In the second half of Book 1 Dido dominates the action, and our admiration for her is evoked to the highest degree. She has courage and resolution, as shown by her successful foundation of Carthage when she was driven out from Tyre (in this respect her task was similar to that of Aeneas and she has already achieved what he is a long way away from); she is as beautiful as Diana; she is highly efficient in organising her people; and she is kind and sympathetic in helping the shipwrecked Trojans ('Being acquainted with grief, I am learning to help the unlucky', 1.630). No happier picture of well-deserved success could have been built up. But already towards the end of Book 1 forebodings of disaster are felt as Virgil tells of Venus' scheme to make Dido fall helplessly in love – a love which we know can have no happy outcome because of Aeneas' commitment to leave for Italy; and did not Dido know this too?

The second section of Dido's tragedy is developed in the first half of Book 4. She now is so wholly absorbed in her passion for Aeneas that she puts from her all other aspects of her personality; she ceases to care for the welfare of the people whose ruler she is, and Carthage grinds to a halt ('all at a standstill' 4.86–9). Through the machinations of Juno and Venus she is deluded into believing that she has been married to Aeneas when they shelter together in a cave. At this point Aeneas is reminded imperiously by Mercury that his divine mission forbids him to stay longer in Carthage, and with a shock of realisation he prepares to leave. Dido speaks to him in a pleading speech whose pathos arouses the deepest sympathy for her: she tells him, as is only too true, that she has given up everything for him, and that losing him she loses everything. Aeneas' reply is cold and heartless (deliberately so, as Virgil indicates several times, because he fears to reveal his love); he tries to convey to her that his divine duty forces him to leave against his personal wishes ('God's will, not mine, says "Italy" ', 4.361).

This closes the second part of the story during which our sympathy for the unhappy queen has been intensely aroused. The final section of the tragedy begins with Dido's reply to Aeneas' rejection of her. Her speech is violently angry, rhetorical, filled with a passionate longing for vengeance: she distances herself entirely from the normal human world and becomes a kind of archetypal figure of hatred and rage. She ceases now to arouse our sympathy, and instead arouses terror. Under the pressure of events which she was not able to resist she has changed from the admirable queen, changed again from the pitiable, rejected lover, and become a personification of madness and revenge. In her final long speech (590ff.) she extends her hatred from the particular to the universal as she calls on all her descendants to show undying hostility to Aeneas' descendants ('I call down a feud between them and us to the last generation!', 629).

In her very last speech before her suicide she shows again these aspects of her character: at first (651ff.) she reviews her achievements and again commands our admiration and our sympathy for her unhappiness, and finally (659ff.) she returns to the theme of vengeance and hatred. After her death the book ends quietly, in the fashion of a Greek tragedy, and the reader is left incredulous that prosperity and virtue can so suddenly turn to calamitous disaster. Was it some fault in Dido's character? Or the irresistable pressure of circumstances? Or a combination of both?

One thing is very certain, and that is that Virgil has portrayed Dido with the utmost sympathy. She could have been depicted as an obstacle to the Roman mission in such a way that the reader would rejoice when she had been swept away (like Calypso and Circe who are obstacles to Odysseus' return in the *Odyssey*), but Virgil has told the story in such a way that it is the tragedy of Dido and not the triumph of the Roman mission which remains in the mind. ✓ 4/08/09

Turnus

Turnus is essentially a hero of the Homeric kind – brave, impetuous, most truly himself on the battlefield, concerned above all with his individual honour. The first reference to him in the poem (6.89) speaks of him as another Achilles, and his deeds of prowess (especially in the second half of Book 9) are wholly in the Homeric spirit. In the final scenes of Book 12

Virgil again and again includes reminiscences of the duel between Achilles and Hector in *Iliad* 22. These aspects of him in many ways win the reader's sympathy, and the view has sometimes been expressed that Turnus is the true hero of the poem.

But for all Turnus' good qualities it must be recognised that Virgil has portrayed him as an essentially violent warrior whose qualities, however appropriate in a heroic age, are not acceptable in a more developed form of society. The word *violentia*, a word with strongly unfavourable connotations, is used only of Turnus in the *Aeneid*; he is very frequently compared with wild animals (lions, tigers, wolves); and his behaviour on occasions (particularly when he kills Pallas, 10.439 ff.) is savage and cruel. His attitude towards the oracles of the gods which oppose him is angry and contemptuous; many of the accusations which Drances, his Italian opponent, throws at him (11.343 ff.) are true. His arrogant self-confidence and his egocentric attitude compel the feeling that in spite of the justifications that can be put forward for him he is too violent a personality to be acceptable in a civilised world. The emblem of a chimaera (dragon) on his helmet marks him out as an archaic and essentially barbaric warrior.

Yet for all that Virgil wins our sympathy for Turnus in his final downfall. However clearly we see that Turnus has brought disaster upon himself by his intransigent attitude, we nevertheless feel for him the kind of pity which a Greek tragedy evokes, and his acceptance of his fate is noble and heroic. The Roman destiny demanded his elimination, but Virgil does not allow the reader to regard this as wholly acceptable. The poem ends with our attention concentrated on the death of Turnus rather than on the triumph of Aeneas.

Minor characters

The three major characters, Aeneas, Dido and Turnus play a far larger part in the poem than any others. But several minor characters are very important in the way in which they represent main themes in the poem. Most prominent of these is Aeneas' father, Anchises, whose role during his lifetime (Books 2 and 3) illustrates the enormous strength of Roman family ties, particularly the father-son relationship. From Anchises, old as he is, Aeneas receives the sort of help and guidance which he himself aims to offer to his son Ascanius, and to Anchises he shows a respect and deference of the kind typical of the Roman ideal of family life. Throughout the long travels recounted in Book 3 Anchises plays a dominant role in decision-making, and his son consults him for advice in all times of crisis; in the anniversary ceremonies after Anchises' death he is shown honour almost, if not quite, as if he were a god; lastly it is Anchises' ghost in the underworld which gives to Aeneas the revelation of future Roman glory which finally strengthens and makes certain his resolution.

We may group together a number of minor characters who illustrate Virgil's extreme sadness at the disaster of youthful death. The slaughter of Pallas in Book 10 and the description of his funeral at the beginning of Book 11 are narrated in the tones of muted sorrow so typical of Virgil: the same is true of the death of Lausus at the end of Book 10, of Camilla at the end of Book 11, of Nisus and Euryalus in Book 9, and of countless other warriors (like Cretheus and Aeolus for example) who appear only briefly. The war-scenes of Book 2 are of this kind, culminating in the death of Priam's son Polites and then Priam himself; the lamentations of bereaved parents (Euryalus' mother, Pallas' father) add to the feeling of deep sorrow at the tragedy of death in battle.

The subordinate commanders of the Trojans are hardly delineated at all – Achates is a shadowy figure, and the same is true of Ilioneus, Sergestus and the rest. In this way the loneliness of Aeneas is accentuated. The subordinates of Turnus again play second fiddle to their commander: the godless Mezentius is vividly portrayed and our sympathy aroused for Camilla at her death, but Messapus, Ufens and the rest are left as vague figures. The contrast with Homer's *Iliad* in this respect is enormous; among the Trojans not only Hector but Sarpedon and Paris are vividly presented, while the Greek forces contain many exciting warriors besides Achilles – Agamemnon, Menelaus, Odysseus, Diomedes, Ajax, Idomeneus, Patroclus and so on.

Finally, King Latinus serves as an extreme foil to the ardent impetuosity of Turnus; he is undecided, wavering and deeply depressed about the situation. His queen, Amata, briefly figures as an unstable character of violent emotion; his daughter Lavinia has no personality at all, and is a part of the plot rather than a character in her own right. It is fair to say that except for Anchises and the young warriors killed in battle Virgil has concentrated the whole of his attention on his three main characters, the hero himself, Dido and Turnus.

Book one

The opening scenes of the *Aeneid* present most of the major themes which are developed in the course of the poem. First and foremost there is the relationship of the *Aeneid* to Homer's *Iliad* and *Odyssey*: Book I of the *Aeneid* follows the episodes of *Odyssey* 5–8 very closely, in such a way as to suggest a comparison between Aeneas and Odysseus, but at the same time Virgil emphasises the differences. Two in particular are highly important - while Odysseus was the great individualist Aeneas is the social man, the man of *pietas* (devotion to duty); and while Odysseus' journey home was a private matter Aeneas' voyage is a public one, divinely inspired as Jupiter indicates in his speech in 254ff.

Secondly the hostility of Juno to the Trojans is powerfully presented, both in the prologue (1–33) and in the scene which follows. Juno symbolises the apparently inexplicable sufferings and disasters which befall a man through no fault of his own, and one of the main problems which Virgil explores in the poem is that of hostile fortune within a world controlled by providence.

Thirdly we have our first glimpses of the character of Aeneas, and the relationship of a man who is following the will of the gods with the gods themselves. He is not portrayed as superhuman because of his divine favour, rather he is frail and sometimes rebellious, only just strong enough, only just resolute enough, to continue with his mission.

Fourthly there are passages, especially from 34–156, which show Virgil's brilliance of mythological description, his verbal music in an unreal world of poetic imagination. The supernatural elements in the poem have, of course, symbolic and

25

religious significance, but it should never be forgotten that they also exist in their own right as part of Virgil's visual imagination; they show us visions which our mortal eyes cannot see.

Finally the second half of the book begins the story of Dido's tragedy, always the most widely-read and widely-remembered part of the poem. In it Virgil expresses his sense of bewilderment and pathos at the suffering inherent in the human condition, suffering which occurs not only in spite of the great world mission of Rome but in this case because of it.

1–7.   The prologue to the poem suggests comparison with Homer, a new *Iliad* ('war') and a new *Odyssey* ('much travailed on sea and land'); it indicates at the same time the great difference between Virgil's poem and those of Homer by the word 'destiny' (2) and the transition from Troy (1) to Rome (7). The major theme of the *Aeneid* is the fulfilment by Aeneas of his divine mission (6) to found a new city from the ashes of Troy which will give the whole world a new civilisation. This task imposed upon him (and so on all the Romans) by fate involves trials and difficulties of all sorts which Virgil symbolises in his poem by means of the hostile goddess Juno (4).

2.   **Lavinian:**   Aeneas' first settlement in Latium was Lavinium; from here the Trojans moved to Alba Longa (7) and thence to Rome. See 270–4.

8–11.   **Where lay the cause . . . ?:**   these lines are an invocation to the Muse (a literal translation of the Latin would be 'Muse, tell me the causes. . .'), based on Homer's invocations at the beginning of the *Iliad* and the *Odyssey*, but differing significantly in that Homer had asked the Muses for the story, but Virgil asks for the causes behind the story, the reasons for the suffering involved in the fulfilment of the will of destiny.

10.   **Piety:**   this word (the Latin noun is *pietas* and its adjective *pius* is frequently applied to Aeneas) means a devotion to duty of every sort, not only to the gods, but to one's country, one's family, one's dependants. It was a specially Roman virtue, one which Aeneas' behaviour in the poem illustrates, but one which also caused problems and disasters (as when *pietas* forces Aeneas to leave Dido and thus cause her to kill herself). The tension between duty and individual desires, and indeed between different kinds of duty, is one of the great themes of the poem.

①

12–33. There was a town of old . . . : a further expansion of the prologue, preliminary to the beginning of the narrative of the poem in 34. It emphasises the hostility of Juno, explaining it partly in a context of Mediterranean history (she favoured Carthage, Rome's great rival in her rise to power) and partly on the mythological grounds of Juno's support for her beloved Greeks against the Trojans in the Trojan war, and her anger against the Trojan Paris who had awarded the prize for beauty to Venus and not to her (27).

12. Men from Tyre: Carthage was founded by settlers from Phoenicia, the chief towns of which were Tyre and Sidon, which frequently form epithets in the *Aeneid* for Carthaginians.

16. Samos: an island in the Aegean which was a special seat of Juno's worship.

28. Her hate for Troy's origin . . . : these additional mythological reasons for Juno's anger refer to the foundation of Troy by Dardanus, son of her husband Jupiter and Electra, and to the attention paid by Jupiter to the handsome Trojan prince Ganymede.

30. The few that the Greeks . . . : Aeneas and his followers were among the few who survived the ten-year war which ended in the sack of Troy by the Greeks. Achilles was the outstanding Greek warrior.

33. So massive . . . : this final line of the prologue summarises in a memorable way the theme of the *Aeneid*: an ancient scholiast remarks, 'for great things are not achieved without great suffering'.

34. Just out of sight of Sicily: Virgil begins the narrative with the Trojans very near their goal in Italy after seven years of wanderings (which are narrated in a 'flash-back' by Aeneas to Dido in Book III).

39ff. Athene: this refers to the vengeance taken by Pallas Athene on Ajax, son of Oileus, for his having violated her priestess Cassandra. Juno complains that lesser deities could take their vengeance on those they hated, but she, queen of heaven, cannot succeed in her desire for vengeance on the Trojans.

52. Aeolia: this passage about the island of Aeolus, king of the winds, is based on a passage in Homer, *Odyssey* 10. It is a brilliant piece of mythological description, the sort of painting in words which Virgil loved to compose.

67. Tyrrhene sea: to the west of Italy, very close to their goal.

81–156. Thus he spoke . . . : the storm scene is presented as a mixture of mythological fantasy and naturalistic description (Aeolus – mighty waves – Neptune).

27

92. **A mortal chill went through Aeneas:** at this first appearance of the hero of the poem we are made to realise that he is a man with the weakness and frailty common to humanity, in no way a superhuman character able to ride all fortune's blows. His ultimate achievement is all the more memorable because he is only just able to achieve it.

96. **Diomed:** the reference is to a single combat, described in Homer's *Iliad*, between Aeneas and Diomedes, one of the greatest of the Greek warriors, from which Aeneas was rescued by his divine mother. He wishes now that he, like so many of his companions (Hector, Sarpedon), had died in the war against the Greeks. Simois was one of the rivers of Troy.

120-1. **Ilioneus ... Aletes:** various Trojan subordinate commanders (Achates is Aeneas' faithful companion, cf. 188), but none of them is of importance in the poem. Aeneas is a very lonely leader of men.

130. **Her brother:** Neptune, like Jupiter, was brother of Juno.

144. **Nereid and Triton:** sea-divinities; notice how the scene ends with a highly pictorial piece of mythological description.

148 ff. **Just as so often ... :** this is the first full length simile in the poem, and carries in it, as so often in Virgil, not merely an immediate point of comparison with the narrative but a relationship with main themes of the poem. The contrast between 'violence' and 'hysteria' (the Latin word is *furor*) and 'goodness of heart' (*pietas*) represents the polarities between which the whole poem operates. It is Aeneas' task by means of *pietas* to conquer *furor* (madness, frenzy, loss of rational control) both within himself and others, a task which he achieves only with very limited success.

A further point which emphasises the importance of this simile is that the comparison is not of the expected kind: normally a simile will compare human activity with the world of nature (Achilles like a lion, the noise of battle like a roaring torrent), but this is the other way round – the storm is calmed as a responsible statesman calms a mob.

195. **Acestes:** a Trojan already settled in Sicily, cf. 550 and 5.30.

198-207. **Comrades ... :** Aeneas' words of comfort are those expected of a leader of men, but notice how Virgil tells us immediately afterwards that his heart was sick with anxiety.

200-1. **Scylla ... Cyclops:** the perils of Scylla and Charybdis and of the Cyclops were described in Homer's *Odyssey* (Books 9 and 12) and Aeneas gives an account of his own encounters with them in Book 3. 554ff.

205. **Destiny offers a home:** again there is emphasis on the fated nature of Aeneas' mission (cf. 2).

220. **True-hearted:** the Latin is *pius*; it is the duty of Aeneas to be deeply concerned about his lost comrades; see note on 10.

223–304. **Jupiter from high heaven ...:** the first of many scenes in Olympus, the home of the gods, with which the mortal story (in Virgil as in Homer) is interwoven. Not only does this piece of epic tradition afford Virgil the opportunity of expressing his visual imagination in a supernatural world, but in a primary sense it conveys his deeply-held belief that the world of divinities and the world of mortals is interrelated. The interrelationship is not as close as in Homer, where gods and goddesses constantly involve themselves – sometimes physically – in mortal events, but it is none the less real for being more symbolic.

228. **Venus:** the mother of Aeneas by Anchises is the protecting divinity of the Trojans, as Juno ('one being', 251) is their implacable opponent.

242. **Antenor:** Venus, as Juno had done (39 ff.), uses an example (of someone permitted to achieve what she is apparently not permitted) in the best Roman oratorical tradition. Antenor, a Trojan, had escaped and established a town for himself and his followers at the head of the Adriatic; why then, she asks, cannot Aeneas do the same?

253. **Being true:** *pietas*. Venus is echoing Virgil's own query in the prologue (10): why must a good man suffer?

257–96. **Fear no more ...:** Jupiter's speech, prophesying a glorious future for the Romans in accordance with destiny, gives a powerful patriotic impulse to the poem early on, and shines through the dark places when the difficulties involved in this mission seem overwhelmingly great and the disasters caused by it (like Dido's death) almost unacceptable. It should be noticed that it is the reader who is heartened by this speech; Aeneas does not hear it, and must make his own faltering way as best he can without any full-scale revelation of the future until the end of Book 6. For an analysis of this speech see Appendix 1.

258. **Lavinium:** the first settlement (cf. 2), so called after King Latinus' daughter Lavinia whom Aeneas married.

259–60. **Exalt ... to the starry skies:** a promise of deification, such as that accorded by the Romans to mortals like Romulus, Hercules, and (after his death) Julius Caesar.

263. **Mightily warring:** this refers to the events in the second half of the *Aeneid*.

264. **City walls and a way of life:** Aeneas' mission was not only

to found a new city in a western land but to set up a new way of life, to leave behind for ever the heroic world of Troy and become the first Roman.

265. **Third summer:**   there was a tradition that Aeneas did not live long after his victory over Turnus and the Rutulians.

267. **Ascanius:**   Aeneas' son Ascanius was also called Iulus: Virgil here links the name etymologically backwards with Troy (Ilium) and (288) forwards with the Julian gens into which the future emperor Augustus was adopted by Julius Caesar.

269 ff. **Ascanius for his reign . . .:**   the chronology of the Trojan-Roman dynasty is three years of rule for Aeneas in Lavinium, thirty for Ascanius in Lavinium and Alba Longa, then three hundred in Alba Longa before the foundation of Rome itself by Romulus. This largely covers the gap between the traditional date of the fall of Troy (1184 B.C.) and the foundation of Rome (753 B.C.).

273. **Priestess:**   the mother of the twins Romulus and Remus was called sometimes Ilia (thus connecting her with Ilium, Troy), sometimes Rhea Silvia, connecting her with the dynasty name of Rome's Alban kings (6.763 ff.).

274 ff. **Twin sons . . .:**   the story of how the twins were suckled by a she-wolf was a very famous piece of Roman legend, often reproduced pictorially on coins (cf. 8.630 ff.). The name Rome was associated with Romulus; that the legend made Mars, god of war, his father is appropriate for the Roman pride in their military achievements.

282. **Togaed:**   the Roman civilian dress was the toga; the point here therefore is not merely one of pride in their national costume, but that they will ultimately exchange their warlike ways for peace.

283 ff. **An age shall come. . .:**   Jupiter cites two periods of future Roman history: the conquest of Greece (which Rome achieved in the second century B.C.), referred to in terms of Aeneas' own heroic age and the names of the Greek leaders who defeated the Trojans; and the reign of Augustus (not Julius Caesar, as some commentators have thought) when the Roman empire would extend to the ends of the earth.

291 ff. **Then shall the age of violence . . .:**   these lines (along with those in 6.847 ff.) constitute the most explicit statement of Rome's destiny: after conquest ('violence') there follows peace for all the world. The ideas of 'Faith', 'the Home', 'the laws' were all important parts of Roman ideals; and the personified figure of 'Discord' (the Latin is *furor*) which will be bound and helpless represents the irrational element in man (see note on 148 ff.) which must be tamed

by devotion to duty (the word 'godless' is a translation of *impia*, 'lacking devotion to duty').

294. **Gates of War:** these were in Janus' temple and had hardly ever been closed in Rome's long history until Virgil's own time in the reign of Augustus.

335 ff. In Venus' account of the story of Dido we notice the many points of similarity with Aeneas' own fortunes –driven from his homeland with the task of founding a new city. Dido has already achieved what Aeneas is trying to do– it is not surprising that the two leaders of their people find much to admire in each other.

378. **I am true-hearted Aeneas:** the heroic tradition was to announce one's identity in simple terms (e.g. 'I am Odysseus, son of Laertes'); here the addition of the epithet 'true-hearted' (*pius*) conveys the same sense of injustice, as Aeneas enumerates his sufferings, as when Venus herself had asked, 'Is this the reward for being true?' (253).

407. **Must you too be cruel?:** the suffering of Aeneas is accentuated by his mother's unfeeling deception of him.

430–6. **So in the youth of summer ...:** the simile of bees portrays organised activity: Virgil had treated this subject fully in *Georgics* 4 (where many of these same phrases had been used), and there are other such similes in the *Aeneid* (6.707 ff., 12.587 ff.).

437. **Ah, fortunate you are ...:** this line summarises the contrast between Dido's Carthage, already founded and being energetically brought to completion, and Aeneas' present plight, shipwrecked and lost in his endeavours to found his city.

444. **The skull of a spirited horse:** the story was that as a result of Juno's oracle the Carthaginians founded their city on a site where they discovered a horse's head, token of victory in war as well as of wealth (cf. 3.539 ff.). Coins of Carthage often showed a horse's head.

450. **Had seen Dido's fear allayed:** it is more likely that the Latin means 'saw Aeneas' fear allayed', a theme on which the next phrase is a variation.

457–8. **The sons of Atreus ...:** these were Agamemnon and Menelaus; Achilles was hostile to them as well as to Priam (king of Troy) since – as the *Iliad* relates – he withdrew from fighting for the Greeks because of his anger with Agamemnon.

462. **Tears in the nature of things:** this phrase (*sunt lacrimae rerum*) is the most often quoted phrase of the *Aeneid*, being used to symbolise the notes of sorrow and pathos that are so often dominant in the poem. A better translation might be 'tears for human happenings': it is most important to realise that the meaning is that

that people show sympathy, not that the world is a vale of sorrow.

466-93.   He beheld scenes ...:   this description of the pictures is called an ecphrasis, a descriptive passage within a narrative framework. The earliest example of it is in Homer, *Iliad* 18, where the newly-made shield of Achilles is described. Other examples in Virgil are the pictures on Apollo's temple (6.20ff.) and the description of Aeneas' shield (8.625ff.). The poetic intention here, apart from the obvious one of varying the narrative and prolonging the suspense as we wait for Dido, is to indicate the suffering which the Trojans had undergone and the ruthlessness of their Greek opponents; it is therefore a prelude to the full description of this in Book 2. The pictures are presented in four pairs: (i) the fleeing Greeks, the fleeing Trojans; (ii) death of Rhesus, death of Troilus; (iii) supplication by the Trojan women, supplication by Priam; (iv) Trojan allies – Memnon's armies, Penthesilea's Amazons. Between (iii) and (iv) Aeneas himself is depicted, and in the whole passage we view the scenes through the eyes of Aeneas.

470.   Rhesus: the story is told in Homer, *Iliad* 10 of how the Greeks Odysseus and Diomedes made a night attack and killed Rhesus when he had just arrived from Thrace to help the Trojans, thus forestalling the oracle that if his horses 'grazed the meadows of Troy' the city would never be taken.

474.   Troilus: the youngest son of Priam who was, in this version of the legend, killed by Achilles; again there was an oracle that if he survived to manhood Troy would not be taken.

479.   Their goddess, their foe's friend: i.e. Pallas Athene who supported the Greeks; there is a description in *Iliad* 6 of how the Trojans tried to placate her.

484.   Ransom: this refers to the last book of Homer's *Iliad* in which the old King Priam went to Achilles, who had just killed Hector, in order to ransom the body.

489-90.   Memnon ... Penthesilea: Memnon came (from Africa) to help the Trojans late in the war, as did Penthesilea, Queen of the Amazon warriors.

496.   Most beautiful to see: already (360-4) Venus has given an idea of Dido's courage and resourcefulness; to this is now added her radiant beauty and (504-8) her powers of government and organisation. Later in this same scene, culminating at 630, a most convincing picture is given of her kindness and sympathy. It is small wonder that Aeneas is led to admire her and fall in love with her.

499.   Diana foots the dance ...:   Diana, the goddess of the hunt ('arrowy one'), is depicted among her mountain-nymphs (Oreads) in

Sparta (whose river was the Eurotas) or Delos, the island of Mt.
Cynthos where she and Apollo were born of Latona. The simile looks
backwards to Aeneas' belief that the disguised Venus might be Diana
(329) and forwards to the simile in 4.143ff. where Aeneas is compared
with Apollo, Diana's twin.

530. **Hesperia:** literally 'the Western land', a frequent word for
Italy in the *Aeneid*.

535. **Rainy Orion:** the constellation Orion was associated with
storms (cf. 4.52, 7.719).

544-5. **Aeneas was our king. . .:** the admiration of Ilioneus for
his leader gives a powerful impression of Aeneas' care for his men,
another aspect of his *pietas* ('duteous of heart').

550. **Acestes:** cf. 195.

569. **Land of Saturn:** Saturnus, king of heaven before his son
Jupiter, was associated with the legendary Golden Age in Latium
where he was said to have taken refuge from his son; cf. *Ecl.* 4 and *Aen.*
8.319ff.

595-610. **I am here, before you . . .:** Aeneas' speech of
gratitude, in the best tradition of Homeric chivalry, is full of tragic
irony in view of the disastrous outcome for Dido of her kindness and
hospitality. The last phrase, 'wherever I am summoned to go' is
particularly significant as it is Aeneas' 'summons' to Italy which
forces him to leave Dido, and causes her death.

613. **Sidonian:** see note on 12.

619. **Teucer:** a Greek exile who went to Cyprus; Virgil here
suggests that in Cyprus he met Dido's father and told him all about
the Trojan war.

630. **Being acquainted:** a most moving line, the culmination of
Dido's sympathetic reception of the shipwrecked Trojans.

650. **Argive Helen:** the abduction of Helen, wife of Menelaus,
by Paris was the cause of the Trojan war. Argive is used in a wide
sense to mean 'Greek' (Argos, like Mycenae, was one of the chief
towns of the heroic age in Greece). Helen was the daughter of Leda
and Jupiter, who came to Leda in the form of a swan. There is a
feeling of foreboding caused by the mention of presents which
originated with Helen.

661. **Tyrian equivocation:** literally 'the two-tongued Tyrians';
the Romans always thought of the Carthaginians as perfidious.

667. **Your own brother, Aeneas:** both Cupid and Aeneas were
sons of Venus, by different fathers.

721. **Sychaeus:** her previous husband (343) to whose ashes she
had made a vow of perpetual widowhood (4.15ff, 552).

732-3. **Grant this be a happy day . . .:** in Dido's final long speech just before her death she makes a different request – that the children of Troy and Carthage may for ever be implacable enemies (4.629).

740.   **Iopas:** a minstrel's song was part of the expected accompaniment of a regal banquet; the minstrel Demodocus sings three times at Alcinous' banquet (*Odyssey* 8). The subject of Iopas' song is reminiscent of the poem of Virgil's great predecessor in hexameter verse, Lucretius.

751.   **The son of Aurora:**   Memnon (see note on 489). In this line and the next it is plain that Dido is asking all the questions she can think of, down to the most precise details.

753.   **But no, dear guest:**   these are Dido's words, as is not quite evident from the translation. 'No' suggests that Dido no longer wants isolated answers to questions, but the whole story; and this is told in the next two books.

Book two

This is perhaps the most intense book of the whole poem. Its action is concentrated into a few hours and it portrays with dramatic immediacy the destruction of a city and the death of many of its occupants, all the more immediate because narrated by one of the survivors.

It is a book in which the concept of destiny is at its strongest: again and again we see that destiny, with the Olympian gods as its agents, has decreed the fall of Troy, and we begin to realise that a new destiny awaits the remnants of the Trojans under Aeneas' leadership, in the foundation of a new city which will one day rule the world.

Aeneas himself is portrayed in the Homeric mode, a warrior ready to make the heroic gesture and sell his life dearly when all seems lost: he is slow to realise that he is not free to do this because of the plan of the gods, and after Hector's prophecy he is still determined to die with his friends; it needs Venus' intervention to persuade him that he must leave the city; and even then when he loses Creusa he puts his life into danger by trying to find her. The supernatural appearance of her ghost finally convinces him, and he 'accepted defeat . . . and made for the mountains' (804).

The book falls very clearly into three sections; the first (1–249) concerned with the story of Sinon, Laocoon and the wooden horse; the second (250–558) with the massacre in Troy culminating in the death of King Priam; and the third (559–804) with the personal fortunes of Aeneas and his family. The loss of his wife Creusa ends the book on the note of tragedy which has been its characteristic throughout.

35

6-7   Myrmidon ... Ulysses: the reference is to the soldiers of two outstanding Greek leaders: first the followers of Achilles, the Myrmidons of Thessaly, and then those of Ulysses (Odysseus) of Ithaca who was responsible with the goddess Athene's help (15) for the strategem of the wooden horse. Even the Greek enemy would weep, Aeneas says, at the tragedy of Troy's destruction.

14.   With so many years: the siege lasted ten years: during this time the Greek ships were drawn up off the coast of Troy and fighting went on in the strip of land between the town and the coast.

21.   Tenedos: an island a few miles off the coast.

29.   Dolopes: Thessalian soldiers associated with Achilles (cf. 6-7).

33.   Minerva: the Roman name for the goddess Pallas Athene (15).

41.   Laocoon: son of King Priam, Trojan priest of Apollo: Virgil was the first to make him a central character in the story of the wooden horse, and the episode which follows (especially its tragic denouement, 199 ff., where see note) is one of the most famous in the *Aeneid*.

49.   Whatever it is ... :   a famous line which became proverbial - *timeo Danaos et dona ferentes*.

54.   Destiny: the emphasis on the fact that Troy's doom was fated is constant throughout this book (33, 247 etc.). The destined foundation of the new city of Rome depended on the old city of Troy being destroyed.

56.   Topless towers: Day Lewis represents the high emotion of these words (note the direct address to the city), with a quotation from Marlowe: 'Was this the face that launched a thousand ships and burned the topless towers of Ilium?'

58.   Young man: Sinon, a Greek who lets himself be captured, pretending to be a deserter in order to fool the Tojans with a false story about the wooden horse. This story of Greek treachery is treated so as to contrast with the friendly and humane attitude of the Trojans who are taken in by it. The rhetoric which Sinon uses is in the highest oratorical style: it is a fine example of a wholly untrue story made convincing by rhetorical trickery.

81.   Palamedes: Sinon's story of internal dissent among the Greeks is based on truth, but that he was involved in it is his own fabrication: notice how he tries to gain sympathy by adding the detail that Palamedes was against the war. His enmity with Ulysses (regarded by the Trojans and Romans as the arch-villain, a Greek with all the worst Greek traits) would of course help his cause. The different attitudes to Ulysses (Odysseus) at different times in literature are brilliantly traced by W.B. Stanford, *The Ulysses Theme.*

100.   **Calchas:**   the Greek priest – the story is resumed in 122 ff. after this deliberate rhetorical pause.

104.   **The sons of Atreus:**   Agamemnon, leader of the Greek army, and his brother Menelaus.

114.   **Eurypylus:**   Sinon's story is that this Greek emissary was sent back to Phoebus Apollo's main prophetic seat at Delphi in Greece. All of this and what follows is pure invention on Sinon's part.

116.   **With human sacrifice:**   this refers to the sacrifice of Iphigeneia by Agamemnon her father in order to gain fair winds for Troy. This legend was the subject of plays by Euripides and was used by Lucretius as an example of the wickedness to which religious beliefs had led.

133.   **The salted meal, the headband:**   these are ritual elements in ancient sacrifice, normally of course associated with animal victims, not humans.

149.   **Truthfully:**   there is very strong irony in Priam's trustfulness towards a man whose story has had not a word of truth in it.

163.   **Pallas Athene:** the goddess who supported the Greeks also had a temple in Troy containing a sacred image of her (called the Palladium) upon which the safety of Troy depended. Sinon suggests that the theft of this image by Diomedes and Ulysses was a sin against Athene which the Greeks hoped to expiate by the offering of the wooden horse. The Trojans should therefore seize it and take it into Troy while the Greeks are absent seeking new omens in Greece (they are really of course only as far away as Tenedos).

189.   **Outraged this offering to Minerva:**   this was precisely what Laocoon had urged.

193.   **Carry Asia in war:**   Sinon suggests that the Trojans would not merely repel the Greek invaders, but themselves make a counter-attack against Greece.

195–8.   **Such was . . .:**   these four lines, concluding the Sinon story, have an awful finality about them, with a crescendo of Greek warriors, ten years, a thousand ships – and finally Sinon.

201 ff.   **Laocoon:**   the death of the Trojan priest (evidently priest of Neptune as well as of Apollo) is now narrated in a passage of vivid pictorial impact, matched in visual art by the famous marble group of Laocoon and his sons caught by the serpents, now in the Vatican. Lessing used this passage in his *Laocoon* (1766) as a basis for his discussion of the relationship between poetry and the visual arts.

246.   **Cassandra:**   daughter of Priam, to whom Apollo gave the

power to prophesy but also imposed the condition that her prophecies would never be believed (cf. 343 ff.).

259 ff. Let the Greeks out . . .:   the Greeks in the horse are in three groups of three, each led by one of the famous Greek generals – Ulysses, Neoptolemus (son of Achilles, grandson of Peleus, also called Pyrrhus, cf. 469 ff.) and Menelaus, brother of Agamemnon. Epeus actually built the horse which Ulysses, inspired by Athene, had devised.

268. It was the hour: this is the beginning of the second section of the book in which Aeneas himself figures prominently.

270 ff. I seemed to behold our Hector . . .:   this vision of the dead Trojan leader comes to Aeneas as he was in death after Achilles had killed him and dragged him round the walls of Troy. The vision has the illogical confusion of a dream: Aeneas like all the other Trojans really knows very well what had happened to Hector but in his vision the cause of Hector's death has vanished from his memory.

275. Arrayed in the armour of Achilles: this refers to Hector's greatest triumph when he killed Patroclus, who had borrowed Achilles' armour, and stripped him of it. This was the climax of the Trojan successes (told in Homer's *Iliad*) when they besieged the Greek ships in the absence of Achilles who was sulking in his tent.

293 ff. Her holy things . . .:   this is the first indication which Aeneas received of his destiny: all he learns here is that it is his task to leave Troy, taking with him the sacred emblems, and found a new city far away. It becomes clear from the narrative which follows that Aeneas has not been convinced by the message, because he endeavours to sell his life dearly in Troy itself. It needs further messages, from Venus, from Creusa, and then (in Book 3) especially from Apollo before he becomes convinced that fate has chosen him to found a new city which will become the greatest in the world.

296. The puissant Vesta: goddess of the hearth, strongly associated with the safety of the home, and with the 'home-gods' (293), the *penates*.

314. Madly I snatch up: the words used here of Aeneas are those which show total lack of rational control (*ratio*); they are *amens, furor, ira*. He yields to the heroic impulse ('death in battle is a fine thing', 317) without any regard to the divinely sent duty which Hector had described to him. He is still behaving as a Homeric hero – he has to learn to step out of the heroic world into a world of new values; he has to learn that his life is not his to throw away.

320. Hallows: a rare word meaning hallowed emblems.

353.   **Let us die:**   again Aeneas is driven by the heroic impulse (see note on 314). The wolf simile conveys wild desperation: it is used later in the poem of Turnus, but not again of Aeneas.

405-6.   **Her burning eyes ... Her eyes:**   this rhetorical repetition was a feature of Alexandrian style, found quite frequently in the *Eclogues*. In the *Aeneid* it is much rarer and all the more effective because it is saved for passages of intense pathos such as this.

414.   **Ajax most vindictively:**   this is Ajax son of Oileus who was the man who had seized Cassandra (see note on 1.39ff.). He is helped by Agamemnon and Menelaus, sons of Atreus (cf. 500), and the Thessalian Dolopes.

428.   **God's ways are inscrutable:**   a more literal translation would be 'it was decreed otherwise by the gods', i.e. one might have thought the gods would have spared the man who was 'most regardful of justice'. The phrase was a Stoic one, conveying their explanation of what seems to humans inexplicable.

433.   **Evading no danger:**   notice again the emphasis on Aeneas' reckless bravery and his disregard of the message Hector's ghost had brought him. One reason for this is Virgil's intention to make it clear that Aeneas' escape from Troy, when so many brave men died, was not due to cowardice.

456.   **Andromache:**   wife of Hector, son of Priam and Hecuba.

469.   **Pyrrhus:**   son of Achilles, also called Neoptolemus (263); he was born in the island of Scyros ('Scyrian brigade', 477).

541.   **He treated me differently far:**   the story is told at the end of Homer's *Iliad* of how Achilles pitied Priam and returned to him the body of Hector; cf. also 1.483f.

547-8.   **A message to my father Achilles:**   i.e. in the underworld. Achilles had been killed by an arrow shot by Paris in the last stages of the war.

557-8.   **A great trunk...:**   there were two versions of the death of Priam, the one which Virgil has used and the other that Priam was beheaded on the shore at the tomb of Achilles. These final lines strangely and memorably conflate the two versions and convey a sense of the emptiness and desolation to which Troy, 'the mistress of Asia once' was now reduced.

559.   **Then first the full horror:**   the beginning of the third and final section of the book, Aeneas' personal fortunes.

562.   **Creusa:**   daughter of Priam, wife of Aeneas.

567-88.   **Yes, I was now ...:**   this passage about Helen, the cause of the war, which is omitted in all the manuscripts, is preserved in the commentary of Servius as an example of a passage excised by Virgil's posthumous literary executors. Its authenticity has been much disputed, but it seems certain that Virgil wrote it, whether or not he would have retained it in his final version. It illustrates the rage and despair of Aeneas, that he should consider satisfying his desire for vengeance by killing a woman. All through this book Virgil has emphasised the fury and recklessness (588, 'insensate fury'; 594, 'ungoverned rage') to which the tragedies of the sack of the city have brought Aeneas, and this serves as a contrast with the more controlled behaviour which Aeneas gradually learns and generally (but not always) shows in the rest of the poem; but it may be that Virgil had decided on second thoughts that this passage pressed his point too far, and therefore he struck it out. A major theme of the poem is the consideration in the person of Aeneas of how far a man of human passions and instinctive emotional reactions can, or should, control these feelings when confronted with what seems unacceptable and unjust.

590. **My gentle mother:** the goddess Venus.

595. **All thought for love:** the literal translation is 'care for us', i.e. for our family.

602. **The gods, the gods, I tell you ...:** this is the strongest statement of the theme which runs all through the book, that the fall of Troy was fated and could not be prevented by Aeneas or anyone else. Therefore he must escape (619).

604 ff. **Look! I shall wipe away the cloud ...:** this vision which Venus shows to Aeneas, of shapes which mortal eyes cannot see, is a most powerful piece of imaginative description, such as Virgil loves to paint especially in supernatural settings. The picture of the great deities in action is vivid and terrifying: Neptune destroying the walls which he himself had helped to build; Juno, the great enemy, at the gates in 'vindictive fury'; Athene, the warrior goddess of the Greeks, with the Gorgon emblem on her shield; Jupiter himself– not depicted – encouraging the destruction. 'Escape then, while you may, my son ...' (619); what else could he do?

643. **To have seen Troy ruined once ...:** this refers to the legend that Troy was sacked by Hercules when the Trojan Laomedon cheated him.

646. **And to bury me – that will not cost them much:** it is more likely that the meaning of the Latin is 'the loss of burial is easy to bear', a statement which in view of the tremendous importance attached to burial in the ancient world is startling and completely unacceptable to Aeneas.

648-9 **Ever since the ruler ...:** the legend was that Anchises was scorched by Jupiter's thunderbolt for boasting of Venus' love for him.

777–8. **Part of the divine purpose:** again, for the last time in this book, the emphasis on fate is repeated.

780. **For you, long exile ...:** Creusa reiterates Hector's message, adding the location of Aeneas' future city, in Hesperia (the Western land) where the Tiber flows (it is called Lydian because the Etruscans, through whose territory it flowed, were supposed to have come from Lydia in Asia Minor).

783. **A royal bride:** this is Lavinia, King Latinus' daughter; the struggle for her hand between Turnus and Aeneas is described in the second half of the poem.

785–7. **I shall not see the proud halls:** she refers to the fate of a captive, serving the Greek soldiers and their women-folk; this she will avoid because she married Aeneas, son of Venus.

788. **Great Mother of the Gods:** Cybele, worshipped especially on Mt. Ida near Troy (801).

792ff. **Three times:** this memorable image is taken from Homer (*Odyssey* 11.206ff, where Odysseus tries to embrace the ghost of his mother), and is repeated in *Aeneid* 6.700ff. of Aeneas trying to embrace the ghost of Anchises.

801. **Dawn star:** the night's horror ends with the dawn of a new day, presaging the dawn of a new civilisation in Italy to replace the lost Trojan empire.

Book three

This book tells the story of Aeneas' long and wearisome wanderings in search of the site of his new city: it contrasts sharply with Book 2, where the action was concerned with the dramatic and terrible events of a single night. Here there is no intensity, just long endurance; the only part of the book in which the emotional pressure rises is the short section concerned with Andromache. Thus the book affords an interlude between the emotional tenseness of the two books flanking it – Book 2 about Troy's destruction, Book 4 about Dido's tragedy. The interest here is intellectual rather than emotional, as the long search and the resolution of Aeneas and Anchises to continue are described.

The book is divided into three sections, each of which is subdivided into three stages: (i) the Aegean Sea, with the landings in Thrace, Delos and Crete; (ii) the seas around Greece, with stages at the Strophades, Actium and Buthrotum; (iii) Italy and Sicily, i.e. Castrum Minervae, Polyphemus and the journey round Sicily. As is Virgil's way (unlike that of Homer) he varies his accounts of landing and departure to avoid any repetition; he varies the length of the episodes (Actium has ten lines, Helenus and Polyphemus each over 100); and above all he varies – in an exciting and somewhat disquieting way – the tone of the episodes. Most are concerned with the real world, and especially with the religious importance of prophecies; but two (the Harpies in the Strophades islands and the Cyclops near Mt Etna) are baroque descriptions of a world of fancy and mythology. Virgil has aimed at varying the Roman itinerary of Aeneas with descriptive glimpses of the fabulous world of the *Odyssey*; he has tried to show that Aeneas is in some ways like Odysseus, but in other ways very different.

5.   **Antandros:**   a mountain, like Phrygian Ida, near Troy.

13 ff.   **Yonder there lay a land ...:**   Aeneas' first landfall on his search for his new city is in the nearby land of Thrace, allies of the Trojans in the Greco–Trojan war. It is not a happy one, with its grim omen of blood welling from the roots of torn-up saplings. It serves to reinforce the feelings of gloom and misery which Aeneas felt after the destruction of Troy, and to indicate how long and hard his task is to be.

45 ff.   **I am Polydorus ...:**   his story is told in the lines which follow; it does not occur elsewhere in classical literature before Virgil. It is imitated by Dante (*Inferno* 13) and Spenser (*F.Q.* 1.2.30 ff.).

73.   **There is a holy island:**   this is Delos, an island in the Aegean believed to be the birthplace of Apollo and Diana; it was beloved of the Nereids' mother (Doris) and Neptune as being one of the most beautiful islands of their domain. The tradition that it was once a floating island is frequently referred to in antiquity. It is selected as Aeneas' second port of call because of its connexions with Apollo, the god of prophecy who plays such a large part in this book.

96.   **First mother:**   this riddling reference to Italy (original home of Dardanus, Troy's founder) is misunderstood by Anchises and taken to mean Crete.

97.   **Here shall your house hold sway:**   this is the first of the many oracular prophecies of future glory for Rome which occur in the poem.

105.   **Here a Mount Ida stands:**   there was a Mt. Ida in Crete as well as the more famous one near Troy (6). This, along with the connexion with Teucer, one of the Trojan ancestors, and with the Great Mother Cybele (who was specially worshipped near Troy) leads Anchises to his erroneous interpretation of Apollo's oracle.

122.   **Idomeneus:**   one of the leading Greek warriors in the Trojan War; the circumstances of his departure from Crete to Italy (401) form the subject of Mozart's *Idomeneo*.

133.   **Pergamea:**   after Pergamum, the name of Troy's citadel.

163.   **Hesperia:**   literally 'the Western land', a frequent word in the *Aeneid* for Italy.

165–6   **Oenotrians ... Italy:**   the Oenotrians were a legendary people of early Italy; according to one tradition, one of their kings was called Italus.

168.   **Iasius:**   a brother of Dardanus. The tradition referred to here is that they both left Italy to found settlements abroad, and Dardanus founded Troy.

170.   **Corythus:**   a city in Italy called after the father of Dardanus.

44

187.   **Cassandra:**   see note on 2.246.

209.   **Strophades:**   these small islands (the fourth stage on Aeneas' journey) are to the west of the Peloponnese.

212 ff.   **Celaeno and her coven of Harpies . . .:**   these fabulous monsters were bird-like creatures with women's faces; their habit was to snatch and pollute the food of their victims, as especially reflected in the story of Phineus, upon whom Zeus sent this punishment. This episode, like that of Polyphemus near the end of this book, has an unreal mythological impact which contrasts strangely with the other episodes in Aeneas' voyage; the influence of Homer's *Odyssey* (in the case of Polyphemus) and of Apollonius Rhodius' *Argonautica* (in this case) has led Virgil to experiment with a mixture of the fabulous and the real.

247.   **Sons of Laomedon:**   Laomedon was a Trojan king who cheated Apollo and Neptune of the agreed price for building the walls of Troy: his name is used by the enemies of the Trojans in a derogatory way.

252.   **Chief of the Furies:**   the Harpies were often identified with the Furies.

257.   **And force you to chew your tables:**   this strange prophecy is fulfilled at 7.109 ff., where the Trojans have just landed in Italy and are having a meal; the food being insufficient they eat the thin platters of bread on which the food was laid out. It was a traditional part of the story of Aeneas; the attribution of the prophecy to Celaeno is Virgil's own.

280.   **On the shores of Actium:**   the Trojans have travelled northwards along the west coast of Greece, past the group of islands which includes Ithaca, the home of their arch-enemy Ulysses, son of Laertes. They land at Actium (the fifth stage in Aeneas' voyage), famous in Virgil's time as the place of Augustus' final victory over Antony and Cleopatra in 31 B.C., which led to the ending of the civil wars and the establishment of the Roman empire. To commemorate his victory Augustus held a great festival of Actian games: the celebration of games here by Aeneas gives a very clear link from the distant past to Virgil's own times.

293.   **Buthrotum:**   this city, further north along the west coast of Greece, is Aeneas' sixth stage, and Virgil dwells on it much longer than on the previous land-falls because of the opportunity it gives him of presenting a prophecy of the future in the mouth of Helenus, the famous Trojan prophet now living at Buthrotum where he had been taken in captivity. He had married Andromache (Hector's widow) after the death of the Greek Pyrrhus (Achilles' son) who had taken Andromache as a prisoner of war to be his wife.

301-2. **Make-believe Simois:** Simois was one of the rivers of Troy; the Trojan exiles have called a local river by this name to remind themselves of home. Cf. 349 ff., where Troy's other river (Xanthus, also called Scamander) is mentioned, and the Scaean Gate, Troy's main entrance.

321. **That maiden daughter of Priam:** this was Polyxena, who was sacrificed on Achilles' tomb, thus avoiding the fate of captivity.

331. **Orestes:** the husband of Hermione.

335. **Chaon:** this Trojan ancestor is not heard of elsewhere.

349. **Miniature Troy:** see note on 301-2.

381. **The Italy you imagine so close:** the north-eastern part of Italy was in fact close (396 f.), but Aeneas has to reach the mouth of the Tiber on the western side, involving the passage round Sicily and north through the Ausonian (or Tyrrhenian) sea, past Lake Avernus, entrance to the underworld (see note on 441), and Circe's island well north of Naples (cf. 7.10 ff.).

391. **A great white sow:** this legend was, like the legend about eating the tables, traditional in the story of Aeneas: the thirty piglets symbolise the thirty years between the foundation of Lavinium, the first settlement, and Alba Longa (its successor). There is also a link between the colour of the sow, and Alba, which in Latin means 'white'. This prophecy is repeated by the god Tiber in 8.43 ff., and fulfilled in 8.81 ff.

402. **Philoctetes:** a notable Greek warrior who founded Petelia in S. Italy.

405. **Veil your head:** the Romans always did this when sacrificing, unlike the Greeks; this is a good example of Virgil's aetiological way of linking the past with the present.

420. **Scylla . . . Charybdis:** these two mythological monsters are described in a famous passage in Homer (*Od.* 12. 73 ff.); by Virgil's time they had been localised in the Straits of Messina between Italy and Sicily. Because of them Aeneas must sail right round Sicily, past Pachynum, the S. E. promontory of Sicily. Milton's description of Sin (*P.L.* 2.653 ff.) is based on Virgil's Scylla:

> About her middle round
> A cry of hell-hounds never ceasing barked
> With wide Cerberean mouths full loud, and rung
> A hideous peal.

441. **Cumae:** Aeneas' arrival at Cumae, just north of Naples, is narrated at the beginning of Book 6. Here he consults the Sibyl (the 'seeress') in her cave ('antre') by Apollo's temple, and descends with

her to the underworld through its entrance at Lake Avernus, very close to Cumae.

444. **Mystic messages:** a reference to the Sibylline books, a collection of oracles('runes') which the Romans consulted at times of great crisis (see note on 6.69f.).

457. **Open her mouth and prophesy:** i.e. not write down her prophecy, but speak it: cf. 6.76.

474. **The prophet of Phoebus:** i.e. Helenus.

476. **Twice saved from Troy's destruction:** the first time was when Hercules destroyed Troy, the second when Aeneas saved Anchises (when Troy was sacked by the Greeks); cf. 2.642ff.

489. **Astyanax:** the son of Hector and Andromache (cf. 2.455ff.). He was hurled to his death from the walls of Troy when the Greeks sacked it.

497. **A Xanthus in replica:** see note on 301–2. Similarly the tired wanderer Aeneas envies Dido the city she has already founded (1.437).

502. **One day, from those sister cities:** i.e. Helenus' city of Buthrotum in Epirus, and Aeneas' Rome on the Tiber. There may be a reference here to the special privileges given to Nicopolis in Epirus, the site of Augustus' camp at the battle of Actium.

506. **The Ceraunian cliffs:** i.e. Acroceraunia, the point in northern Greece for the shortest sea-passage to Italy.

531. **Minerva's Height:** Castrum Minervae in Calabria (S. Italy) had a famous temple to Minerva ('Athene', 544). This seventh stage on Aeneas' journey is briefly narrated; it is Greek territory and the Trojans leave very quickly after making the appropriate religious sacrifices.

551f. **Next we raised the gulf of Tarentum:** the Trojans are proceeding south-west from the heel to the toe of Italy: Tarentum, the chief town of that area, claimed to have been founded by Hercules. The Lacinian goddess is Juno, who had a famous shrine at Lacinium in this area; Caulonia and Scylacaeum also were towns on this coast.

554. **Trinacrian Aetna:** the great volcano is called Trinacrian because Trinacrian ('with three promontories') was an epithet of the triangular island Sicily.

558. **Charybdis:** the whirlpool in the Straits of Messina, see note on 420.

569ff. **The Cyclops...:** this eighth stage on the journey is told at length. These one-eyed giants, of whom the most famous was Polyphemus, had been encountered by Odysseus (Homer, *Odyssey* 9.106ff.), and Virgil brings his account into close relationship with

Homer's story by many verbal imitations and by the fact that the Greek castaway whom the Trojans meet (Achemenides, 614) had been left behind by Odysseus. In Homer the Cyclops are shepherds living on a small island, but by Virgil's time they had long been localised at Mt. Etna, where as servants of the fire-god Vulcan they worked at their forges (6.630f., 8.418ff.). Here they are presented in their Homeric aspect.

578.   **Enceladus:**   one of the giants who rebelled against Jupiter and, like his fellow giant Typhoeus, was struck down by a thunderbolt and buried under a volcano.

611.   **A gesture of immediate good-faith:**   notice the kindness of the Trojans to their suppliant, even although he is a member of the hated Greek race who had destroyed Troy.

613.   **I am of Ithaca:**   Achemenides came from the same island as Ulysses (Odysseus); in his speech he tells again the story so well-known from Homer of how Odysseus escaped from Polyphemus' cave. There is no mention in Homer of any survivors being left behind by Odysseus; here in Virgil the episode is invented in order to bring into the story of Aeneas' wanderings a sustained imitation of the fantastic world of the *Odyssey* which had cast its spell upon him as it has on all its readers.

681.   **Juppiter's own tall wood:**   the oak groves at Dodona in N. Greece were sacred to Jupiter; Diana, the huntress, was naturally associated with groves.

687.   **Slanting from Cape Pelorus:**   i.e. from the north-eastern tip of Sicily (411). This wind takes them south past coastal towns on the east side of Sicily.

692ff.   **Over against wave-worn Plemyrium ...:**   on this last stage, the ninth, Virgil describes briefly some of the most famous towns of Sicily, many of which would be well-known to his Roman readers. Plemyrium and Ortygia are in the bay of Syracuse; the legend was that the river-god of the river Alpheus in southern Greece fell in love with the nymph Arethusa, and pursued her under the sea to her fountain at Syracuse.

698-9.   **Helorus ... Pachynus:**   places on the eastern side of Sicily.

700-3.   **Camarina ... Gela ... Acragas:**   places on the south coast of Sicily. Each is given just the briefest description.

705-7.   **Selinus ... Lilybaeum ... Drepanum:**   Selinus and Lilybaeum are further west along the south coast of Sicily; Drepanum is on the west coast.

710.   **Lost Anchises:**   the legend about the death of Aeneas' father varied considerably; Virgil has adopted a version suitable for

the inclusion of the story of Dido and for Aeneas' return visit to Sicily in Book 5, where the anniversary celebrations and games at Anchises' tomb are described.

Book four

The fourth book, always the most widely-read part of the *Aeneid*, completes the tragic story of the love of Dido and Aeneas which was begun in Book 1. In the scenes there Virgil had emphasised the admirable qualities of the Queen of Carthage, her courage, her initiative, her beauty, her sympathy. In this book we see first how her passion for Aeneas consumes her whole personality, so that Carthage grinds to a halt and she can think of nothing but her desire to win him; and subsequently, when he has told her that he must leave, we see how she changes from a human personality into a terrifying personification of hatred, fury and vengeance.

Virgil's story of Dido was largely his own creation. There may have been traces of it in early Roman poetry, but it did not form part of the normal version of the Aeneas legend. Virgil has to some extent used the Medea of Apollonius and the Ariadne of Catullus as sources, but his primary source has been the concept of the tragic hero or heroine of the Greek stage – a great and virtuous person brought from prosperity to total destruction by an inherent flaw of character, or by the pressure of irresistible circumstances, or by a combination of both. These were the terms in which Virgil conceived the tragedy of Dido, and he has so constructed it that our sympathy is deeply aroused for the victim of Rome's imperial mission. Dido could easily have been brushed aside as an 'obstacle' to the fulfilment of Rome's destiny, but all readers of *Aeneid* 4 know that Virgil has presented it otherwise. Our intellectual judgment must approve of Aeneas' decision to place his divine mission above his personal inclinations, but our memory lingers not on this triumph for Rome but upon the unhappy victim.

11.   **How powerful in chest and shoulders**:   a better inter-pretation of the Latin is 'how strong in heart and prowess'.

17.   **Since that first love of mine proved false**:   Dido refers to her dead husband Sychaeus (murdered by her brother Pygmalion, see 1.343 ff.): his murder 'cheated' her love and frustrated her hopes of happiness.

18.   **Taken a loathing**:   she had vowed eternal chastity to the ashes of Sychaeus (27, 552).

36.   **Iarbas**:   one of Dido's suitors in Africa (see 196 ff.).

43.   **Tyrian aggression**:   in addition to attack from neighbouring African tribes there is the threat of an invasion by Dido's brother Pygmalion from Tyre. Anna argues that Dido needs Aeneas for military as well as personal reasons.

69 ff.   **Like a doe ...**:   in addition to the direct point of comparison (Dido is driven distracted by the arrow of love) there are other implied similarities with the narrative. The 'deathly shaft' suggests the tragic outcome of the arrow's penetration for Dido as for the doe; the word 'unwary' suggests how Dido too was taken off her guard by the arrows of Cupid; the words 'all unknowing' suggest the failure of Aeneas to recognise the true intensity of Dido's love for him.

84.   **She keeps Ascanius**:   this, like the previous line, refers to Dido's imaginings.

86–9.   **Work on the half-built towers... standstill**:   these lines represent vividly the extent to which Dido has abandoned all other concerns, put off her royal responsibilities and destroyed the rest of her personality in her all-consuming passion for Aeneas.

90 ff.   **Now as soon as Juppiter's consort ...**:   the goddesses Juno and Venus here scheme against each other for their own ends, entirely regardless of the fate of the humans whom they are manipulating. Venus is in much the stronger position because she knows that Jupiter will not approve Juno's plan of miscegenation (112) between Trojans and Carthaginians: it is destined that the Trojans and Italians are to be the ancestors of the Roman race (229).

115 ff.   **That shall be my task ...**:   the translation well brings out the awful matter-of-fact phraseology which Juno uses in describing her plan.

127.   **Hymen**:   the god of marriage.

143 ff.   **It was like when Apollo ...**:   the elaborate comparison of Aeneas with Apollo reminds us of the comparison of Dido with Diana in 1.498 ff.

162–3.   **The grandson of Venus**:   the young Ascanius.

166.   **In the same cave:**   observe how the plans of Juno are fulfilled to the letter (124).

166-8.   **Primordial Earth . . .:**   these supernatural powers reflect the hallucinations of Dido as she imagines that a real wedding ceremony is taking place: the ceremony is inaugurated ('gave the signal') by Earth and Juno, the lightning flashes are the wedding torches, the firmament itself is witness, the Nymphs sing the bridal song.

172.   **Marriage, she called it:**   Virgil here has intervened in the narrative to make it plain that Dido is deluded. We are to understand that when Aeneas says ('nor did I offer you marriage at any time', 338) his words are strictly true. Aeneas' guilt lies not in any broken promises but in not having realised earlier that when he had to depart (as he must have known he would have to) Dido would not be able to live without him.

173 ff.   **Straightaway went Rumour . . .:**   this personification with its sustained descriptive imagery shows Virgil's grandiose style at its best, providing a diversion of a most memorable kind from the narrative of the human actors.

178.   **Mother Earth:**   Earth was the mother of the Giants and Titans (such as Enceladus and Coeus) who rebelled against Jupiter and were destroyed.

196.   **Iarbas:**   one of Dido's African suitors (cf. 36), descended from Ammon (the African name for Jupiter).

216.   **Phrygian bonnet:**   the accusation of effeminacy against the Trojans (Paris especially was regarded by their enemies as an elegant fop) is made elsewhere in the poem by the Italians Numanus and Turnus.

228.   **Rescue him twice:**   once from Diomedes (*Iliad* 5.311 ff.), and once from burning Troy (*Aeneid* 2.589 ff.).

231.   **The whole world under a system of law:**   this aspect of Rome's mission for the world was one on which they rightly prided themselves.

242.   **His magic wand:**   the *caduceus* with which Mercury was often portrayed. One of his functions was escorting the shades of the dead.

244.   **Seals up:**   the meaning here has been disputed, but should almost certainly be 'unseals': the eyes were opened after death, so that the ghost could see during its journey to the underworld.

258.   **His mother's sire:**   a reference to Maia, daughter of Atlas and mother of Mercury.

279 ff.   **Dazed indeed . . .:**   the effect of Mercury's message upon Aeneas is immediate, and his reaction to it equally immediate: he is

in no doubt whatever that he must obey. This divine intervention may be viewed in various ways. Virgil has presented it in visual and mythological terms, with the god appearing in person to Aeneas; we may if we wish discard the pictorial terms and instead say that Aeneas has suddenly become aware of a divine voice speaking to him, or has heard the voice of God; or even that Aeneas' guilty conscience pricks him. At all events he has a sudden recognition that his way of behaviour has been wrong and must be changed.

290.   **Be prepared to fight:**   it is more likely that the phrase means 'prepare the tackle', i.e. on the ships, to make them ready for sailing.

295.   **With cheerful alacrity:**   the Trojans are delighted to be on the move; thus Virgil emphasises the dilemma and the loneliness of Aeneas who has to break the news to Dido.

301.   **Like some Bacchante:**   the female revellers at rites in honour of Bacchus (especially associated with Mt. Cithaeron in Thrace) performed their worship in a wild and orgiastic fashion, with the emotions completely dominating the rational faculties. This is the case with Dido now, as also later with Queen Amata of whom Bacchic imagery is used (7.385 ff.).

314 ff.   **Am I your reason . . .:**   after her angry outburst at the beginning of her speech Dido now pleads with Aeneas; the feeling which Virgil arouses, of sorrow at her plight, is overwhelmingly strong.

320 ff.   **Because of you . . .:**   all these statements are only too true; Dido has burnt all her boats.

332 ff.   **In the end he managed to answer. . .:**   Aeneas' speech is cold and heartless, because he has to be 'mindful of Jove's words' and therefore must 'repress his feeling for her'.

335.   **Elissa:**   Dido's other name.

337-8.   **I did not look . . . marriage:**   both of these statements are true, but that does not help Aeneas' efforts to explain.

345.   **Apollo:**   the various prophecies inspired by Apollo were recounted in Book 3 to Dido, so she was well aware of them, though she chooses to ignore or ridicule them.

351-3.   **Often as night. . .:**   we have not heard elsewhere of these dreams; Aeneas is now aware, as he should have been before, of the indications he has had that he must not stay in Carthage.

361.   **God's will, not mine, says 'Italy':**   this is the essence of the situation. To Aeneas it seems overwhelmingly convincing, as he sets duty above love. To Dido it seems meaningless, concerned as she is with the individual's happiness.

362.   **All the while he was speaking:**   this is the turning point in

the story of Dido. She now puts off all her human qualities, and the speech which follows is rhetorical and distanced, like an orator speaking to an audience rather than a person speaking to another person. It is the essence of her tragic downfall that the pressures to which she has been subjected have changed her from a great and glorious queen to a kind of symbol of hatred and vengeance.

365.   **No goddess mothered you:**   the denial of human (or divine) parentage, the suggestion of birth from rocks or wild animals, was a rhetorical commonplace.

369.   **Not one sigh from him:**   observe how Dido stops addressing Aeneas, and refers to him in the third person, as someone no longer present. Her remarks are addressed to whatever powers of vengeance there be.

379 ff.   **Oh, of course this is just the kind of transaction . . .:**   here Dido speaks Epicurean sentiments, countering the Stoic arguments of Aeneas about divine duty with the Epicurean argument that the gods do not care about humans and play no part in the mortal world at all, living in a calm world of their own.

387.   **The tale of your punishment:**   Dido wants not only vengeance, but the knowledge that she has had vengeance.

393.   **But the god-fearing Aeneas:**   Virgil here gives Aeneas the epithet (*pius*) which is applied to him so often in the poem. It has special force here, being essential to justify Aeneas' conduct. There can be no other adequate reason for his desertion of Dido than the one which he had tried to give, and which is reiterated here: his devotion to the gods in accordance with whose will he is trying to carry out a divine mission.

395-6.   **His heart melting from love of her, nevertheless . . .:**   here is the essence of the human conflict in Aeneas. He is deeply in love with Dido (though he had tried to conceal his love in his reply to her), but he decides he must follow his higher loyalty.

412.   **Excess of love . . .:**   Virgil has already intervened in his narrative in the previous lines to address Dido ('Ah, Dido, what did you feel . . .?'); this second intervention, in which he reflects on the power of love's tyranny, directly invites the reader's sympathy for his heroine.

419-20.   **If I was able . . .:**   the words are ambiguous: Anna assumes she was able to anticipate and so will be able to bear it – but the reader knows she means that she was not able to anticipate it.

425-7.   **Say that _I_ never conspired . . . :**   Dido indicates that she is not a natural enemy of the Trojans – she did not join the Greek naval expedition which assembled under Agamemnon at Aulis in northern Greece to attack Troy; her reference to desecrating Anchises' ashes is an imaginary crime which, had she been guilty of it, would have justified Aeneas' hostility.

436. **My death shall be his interest:** the Latin is highly ambiguous; a more literal translation might be, 'I will repay it in full measure at my death'. What Dido means is deliberately left unclear.

449. **Resolute, though, was his mind:** the simile has portrayed Aeneas as a Stoic, firmly anchored on the rock of his resolution, battered by circumstances but not moved from his purpose.

469 ff. **Just so does the raving Pentheus...:** the double simile refers to famous Greek stories often enacted on the tragic stage – the madness of Pentheus in Euripides' *Bacchae* and the pursuit of Orestes by the Furies after he had killed his mother in revenge for her murder of his father Agamemnon (a story of which the most famous representation is Aeschylus' *Oresteia* trilogy). The impact of these two similes is to liken Dido to a tragic heroine of the Greek stage, brought from happiness to disaster by a mixture of circumstances and character. Notice how this is pointed in 471 by the words 'just so on the stage...'.

493. **Her magic arts:** by her use of magic Dido is associated with the arch-magician Medea, heroine of Euripides' *Medea*, whose patron goddess was Hecate (511).

542. **Laomedon's people:** Laomedon was an ancestor of the Trojans who cheated the gods of their reward for building Troy's walls (see 3.248).

545. **Sidon:** the two Phoenician towns Tyre and Sidon are used interchangeably by Virgil; Dido refers to her homeland from which she was driven by the hostility of her brother Pygmalion.

552. **Memory of Sychaeus:** see notes on 17 and 18.

584–629. **And now was Aurora...:** for an analysis of this passage see Appendix 2.

598–9. **Totes round his home-gods...:** Dido refers to Aeneas' mission of bringing his home-gods safely out of burning Troy, and rescuing his old father Anchises.

600–2. **Torn up his body ... banquet on?:** two of the most horrible of Greek myths: Medea tore her brother Apsyrtus into pieces and scattered the limbs on the sea to delay the pursuit; Atreus served up to Thyestes at a banquet the flesh of his sons.

610. **Elissa:** Dido's other name, cf. 335.

622 ff. **Let you, my Tyrians...:** after the specific curses directed at Aeneas, Dido ends with a wider application of her hatred and desire for vengeance. The course of history fulfilled her prayers,

as the Romans and Carthaginians fought each other for Mediterranean supremacy in the third and second centuries B.C., and the 'avenger' (625) in the person of Hannibal very nearly destroyed Rome for ever in the years 217 and 216 B.C.

651–8.   **O relics of him . . .:**   this part of Dido's last words recalls the first two stages in her tragedy: the achievements of her life, presented in Book 1, and the pathos of her unhappy love, described in the first half of this book.

659–62.   **Shall I die unavenged? . . .:**   the second part of Dido's last words portrays the third and final stage of her story in which she has become a terrifying figure of hatred and vengeance.

682–8.   **You have destroyed more than your self . . .:**   this is only too true. Dido's decision to kill herself has been an abdication of responsibility.

Book five

The fifth book (like the third) lowers the emotional tension between two books of the highest intensity: concerned as it is largely with the description of athletic contests, it introduces a brief feeling of relaxation between the tragedy of Dido's death and the disaster of the burning of the ships which motivates Aeneas' visit to the mysterious and terrifying world of the dead. The book is carefully structured so that the tension gradually diminishes before the beginning of the games, and gradually increases after their end. The first hundred lines or so are concerned with the arrival in Sicily and then with the solemn religious ceremonies; after the last contest in the games the description of the equestrian cavalcade with its strong contemporary associations and its formal beauty prepares the reader for the resumption of the narrative. The intervention of Juno and the burning of the ships reduce Aeneas to the lowest state of despondency (see note on 702), and the book ends with the moving account of the death of the faithful helmsman Palinurus, introducing a note of sorrow which naturally leads in to Book 6.

The games themselves are based on the Homeric precedent in *Iliad* 23, and they also have special contemporary interest in that Augustus had revived interest in the Greek type of athletic contest in the Roman world, especially by the great Actian games he had recently celebrated in honour of his victory at Actium. Virgil has reduced the number of games described in Homer (from eight to four) and has substituted for the Greek élan (which no Roman could hope to capture) a careful symmetry of description and a variety in the interest. The boat-race is long (130 lines) and exciting, full of incident; the footrace is short and centres on a single incident; the boxing (again long, 123 lines) is almost mythological in its presentation; and finally the shorter archery contest ends in a miraculous omen. The announcement of the contests and the award of the prizes are varied both in length and method, and the impression left is one of carefully organised symmetry and elegance of presentation.

4.   **Why so big a fire:**   the Trojans had left Carthage before Dido's suicide, so they conjecture the reason for the flames.

23.   **Your brother Eryx:**   Eryx was the son of Venus and Butes, and therefore Aeneas' half-brother. The well-known mountain and town in western Sicily were called after him.

30.   **Acestes:**   a Trojan living in Sicily, mentioned at 1.195.

31.   **My father, Anchises:**   he had died when the Trojans had reached Sicily, just before they were driven to Carthage (3.709 ff.).

60.   **Yearly to hold these rites:**   this is an anticipation of the annual Roman festival, the Parentalia, in honour and memory of parents.

66.   **A Trojan Games:**   athletic contests traditionally formed a part of funeral celebrations, as for Patroclus in *Iliad* 23.

72.   **His mother's myrtle:**   the myrtle was sacred to Venus.

95–6.   **His father's familiar or the genius of the place:**   there is little difference between these two interpretations: the snake represents Anchises' spirit ('familiar') appearing at his tomb. 'The genius of the place' means the deity of the particular locality (in the Roman pantheistic religion every place had its own local deity).

97.   **Two sheep ... heifers:**   these offerings suggest the well-known Roman sacrificial lustration called the Suovetaurilia (a word compounded of the Latin words for pig, sheep and bull).

114.   **A rowing race:**   no other ancient epic has a ship-race in the games. It is appropriate here because so much of the poem has been concerned with sea-faring. Some of its incidents are based on the chariot-race in *Iliad* 23, the first and longest of the contests at Patroclus' funeral games: Virgil acknowledges this with his chariot simile (146 ff.).

116 ff.   **Commended by Mnestheus ...:**   three of the four ship captains have names which Virgil connects etymologically with famous Roman clans (the Memmii, the Sergii, the Cluentii).

192–3.   **Gaetulian quicksands ... Malea:**   places which the Trojans had come through on their voyage: the Gaetulian quicksands were off Carthage (1.102 ff.), the storm in the Ionian Sea was described in 3.192 ff., Cape Malea (the southernmost tip of Greece) was proverbially dangerous.

240-1. Nereids ... Portunus: the picture of these sea-deities rounds off the exciting narrative of the race with an attractive and other-wordly mythological touch.

252 ff. Woven upon it ...: the picture on the cloak is in two scenes, the first showing the young Trojan prince at his favourite occupation of hunting, and the second showing the eagle snatching him up to be Jupiter's cup-bearer in heaven.

291. A running race: this second contest is again based on *Iliad* 23, the running race in which Ajax slips and is therefore passed by Odysseus.

294. Nisus and Euryalus: these two friends play a large part in the war scenes of Book 9.

338. A popular winner: modern ideas of sportsmanship would differ. The later epic writer Statius, imitating this passage, goes one better and has the potential winner held back by his flowing locks so that someone else can win.

364. A boxing match: Roman boxing was a brutal sport, in which the contestants wore heavy gloves reinforced with metal. Virgil clearly had no love for this kind of brutality, and has therefore presented the contest in a mythological way, with the two contestants (who do not figure elsewhere in the *Aeneid*) depicted as giant figures, like Titans from a legendary past.

372-3. Butes ... Amycus: this Butes is not heard of elsewhere; Amycus was the famous boxer king of the Bebrycii in Asia Minor.

392. Eryx: a famous Sicilian boxer (see note on 24). He fought against Hercules (410), but was defeated and killed.

483. Eryx, this better life: the bullock acts as a scapegoat for Dares.

496. Pandarus: the reference is to the Trojan archer who, at Athene's instigation, broke the truce in *Iliad* 4.72 ff.

522. A startling phenomenon: the significance of this omen has been much debated. Many commentators think that it is a reference to the comet which appeared in 44 B.C. and was considered to indicate the reception of Julius Caesar's spirit into heaven as a god; but it seems more likely, as it has such direct reference to Acestes, that it portends the future fame of his city Segesta (see note on 718).

553 ff. Now the boys ride in ...: the cavalry tournament, which concludes the games with a show-piece of pageantry, is the first celebration of the Trojan Game (602) which was a favourite spectacle in Rome in Virgil's time, having been revived by Julius Caesar and established as a regular institution under Augustus, whose wish it was to encourage physical activities among the youth of Rome. Virgil's description is very elaborate and pictorial: he enjoys pausing on this highly visual spectacle.

569. **Young Atys:** Augustus' mother belonged to the Atii, so that there is special point in the friendship of Atys and Ascanius (into whose family, the Julii, Augustus was adopted by Julius Caesar).

588 ff. **It was like the fabled Labyrinth . . .:** the simile of the Labyrinth, which was the home of the Minotaur (see note on 6.25) gives a mythological picture of the intricacy of the movements; the following simile of the dolphins reinforces this idea from the natural world.

604 ff. **At this point, fickle Fortune changed sides . . .:** after the games and the pageant are over, the narrative resumes with an immediate and sudden indication of disaster, caused by Juno through her messenger Iris, goddess of the rainbow.

662 ff. **The Fire-god gallops . . .:** the episode of the burning of the ships was a traditional part of the Aeneas legend; it was normally located in Italy, but by changing to Sicily Virgil has been able to associate Sicily (and the resultant founding of Segesta) very closely with the Roman mission.

700 ff. **But lord Aeneas . . .:** here we see Aeneas at the lowest point of his confidence and resolution. The disaster of the burning of the ships, coming so soon after the brief relaxation during the games, is almost too great for him to bear. The Stoic platitudes of Nautes do not convince him, and it needs the appearance of his father's ghost, sent by Jupiter, to persuade him that he must continue. It is here that Virgil gives the most explicit indication of the relationship between divine destiny and individual free will: he makes it plain – as it indeed has been often enough through the poem, though not so precisely stated – that Aeneas is free to forget his destiny at any time he wishes. It is through the decision of his free will, at each new crisis, that he resolves – often by the narrowest of margins – that he should continue onwards with his mission.

718. **Acesta:** this was the Greek name of the famous Sicilian city which the Romans called Segesta.

732-3. **Death's kingdom . . . Avernus:** Aeneas' visit (accompanied by the Sibyl) to the underworld, and his journey through it to Elysium, is described in Book 6. Avernus is the name of the lake near Naples where the entrance to the underworld was said to be: sometimes the word is used for the underworld itself.

755. **The city's circumference:** i.e. the new city of Segesta.

789-91. **What a wild riot of waters . . .:** a reference to the storm off Sicily which drove the Trojans off course to Carthage (1.81 ff.).

797. **Laurentine Tiber:** the Laurentine territory extended southwards from the river Tiber.

799. **Saturn's son:** Neptune, like Jupiter and Pluto, was a son of Saturnus.

801. **Where you were born:** Venus was born from the sea, near Cythera, an island off southern Greece.

808 ff. **I carried off in a hollow cloud ...:** this is described in *Iliad* 20.318 ff.

811. **Perjured Troy:** Neptune and Apollo were cheated by the Trojan king Laomedon of the agreed price for building the walls of Troy.

813. **Cumae:** near Lake Avernus, where Aeneas makes landfall at the beginning of Book 6.

814. **One only shall you miss:** the story of Palinurus' loss overboard is told in 838 ff.

823–6. **The antique school of Glaucus ...:** Virgil here uses the evocative power of Greek proper names to conclude his description of Neptune's chariot and retinue of sea-deities.

838. **Sleep:** the concept of Sleep as a god is frequent in ancient art and literature from the time of Homer (*Iliad* 14.231 ff.).

848–51. **Are you asking me to forget ...?:** the pathos of this episode is greatly increased by the emphasis on Palinurus' loyalty and devotion to duty, his refusal to trust the 'devilish' deception of the sea.

854. **Lethe ... Stygian:** Lethe (river of forgetfulness) and Styx were rivers of the underworld.

864. **The Sirens:** the story of the maidens who by their song charmed sailors to destruction is told in Homer, *Odyssey* 12.39 ff. By Virgil's time their one-time home was commonly located in the islands called Sirenusae near Capreae. They were no longer a danger because after Odysseus had escaped them they killed themselves. Only the white bones of those whom they destroyed now marked the island.

870–1. **Too easily trusting ...:** the pathos is increased by the irony of this false assumption by Aeneas. The lack of burial was thought in the ancient world to prevent (or delay for a long time) the passage of the ghost of the dead to his rightful place in the after-life. In Book 6 (322 ff) Aeneas meets the ghost of Palinurus, prevented by lack of burial from crossing the Styx.

Book six

This book is central in many ways to the whole significance of the *Aeneid*, and it contains some of Virgil's very finest poetry. It falls naturally into three parts: the first (1–263) tells of the preparations for the descent to the underworld, with strong emphasis on religious rites and sacrifices; the second (264–636) narrates Aeneas' journey through the underworld and his meetings with ghosts of his past; the last section contains the 636– meeting with Anchises in Elysium, his exposition of life after 901 death and his account of the famous Romans waiting to be born.

There are three special reasons why this book is central in its importance: it contains much of Virgil's own religious thought ① displayed partly in the richly coloured mythology of the underworld but mainly in Anchises' speech (724–751); it has one of the greatest patriotic passages of the whole poem (756– ② 853) in which future Roman heroes are described and the Roman mission of peace and government is proclaimed; finally and perhaps most importantly it is crucial in the ③ development of Aeneas' character. Before the descent to the underworld he had often been frail and uncertain in resolution; during the journey to Elysium he is backward-looking, filled with grief and remorse at the disasters of the past, overwhelmed by the suffering of others (Palinurus, Dido, Deiphobus) in which he had been involved; but finally Anchises' revelation of the Roman future which Aeneas must inaugurate strengthens him, makes him confident and determined that he will not fail. Now at last there can be no more hesitation: Anchises has 'fired his heart with passion for the great things to come' (889).

2.   **Euboean Cumae:**   Cumae was an ancient Greek settlement a few miles north of Naples founded by colonists from Chalcis in Euboea; it was the site of Apollo's temple, presided over by his priestess Deiphobe, the Sibyl, and it was close to Lake Avernus, the legendary entrance to the underworld. The ruins of Apollo's temple still stand on the Acropolis of Cumae, and close at hand the Sibyl's cave has been discovered and excavated.

11.   **Sibyl:**   see note on 2. A feature of her prophecies was their wild ecstatic nature when she was possessed by the god (47 ff., 77 ff.).

13.   **Diana:**   the sister of Apollo who shared with him this sacred site.

14.   **Daedalus:**   the master craftsman of legend, here the inventor of the maze (27) in which the Cretan King Minos kept the monster called the Minotaur. No one could escape from the maze, but Daedalus in pity for the princess Ariadne who had fallen in love with Theseus – one of the Athenians sent as yearly tribute (21) to be sacrificed to the Minotaur – showed her how to ensure Theseus' safety by the device of the thread (30–31). Consequently Daedalus had to flee from the wrath of King Minos; this he did by the invention of wings. As is his way, Virgil refers very allusively to the well-known legend.

20 ff.   **On its door . . .:**   this description of the pictures on the door of Apollo's temple is of the type called ecphrasis, i.e. a description of a work of art set within a narrative poem. Other outstanding examples in Virgil are the pictures on Dido's temple (see note on 1.466 ff.) and the scenes on Aeneas' shield (8.626 ff.). The intention of such passages is sometimes purely descriptive, but Virgil's use of it generally involves some thematic link with the narrative; here the connection is between Daedalus' maze and the maze-like wanderings Aeneas has to undertake in the world below. The maze as a symbol of the afterlife was frequently depicted on Etruscan tombs.

20.   **Androgeos:**   a son of Minos who was killed while in Athens. It was as a punishment for this that the Athenians had to pay their yearly tribute to the Minotaur.

24.   **Pasiphae:**   Minos' queen who was punished for a sin against the gods by being forced to conceive a passion for a bull: from this 'monstrous union' was born the Minotaur (half-human, of the race of Minos, and half-bull: *taurus* is the Latin for a bull).

31.   **Icarus:**   son of Daedalus who was fitted out by his father with wings, but flew too near the sun; the wax fastening of his wings was destroyed, and he fell into the Aegean Sea and was drowned.

35. **Trivia:** Diana, goddess of cross-roads, see note on 12.

42. **Cave:** see note on 2. One of its features is the large number of slits in the side of the rock(mouths) from each of which the Sibyl's prophecies emerged.

56. **Phoebus:** Phoebus Apollo was always the great supporter of Troy; he was also the god of expeditions and colonies who was Aeneas' guide during the wanderings described in Book 3.

58. **Paris:** the son of Priam, a famous archer who killed Achilles in the last year of the war by shooting him in the one vulnerable part of his body, the heel by which he had been held when Thetis his divine mother had dipped him into the waters of the Styx to make him invulnerable.

60. **Massylian... Syrtes:** this refers to the coast of Africa off which the Trojans were shipwrecked (1.81 ff.).

63. **Gods and goddesses all:** after invoking his guardian deity Phoebus Apollo, Aeneas now appeals to the deities hostile to Troy, especially Juno and Athene.

69-70. **Temple of solid marble ... festival days:** this has reference to actual events in Rome. Augustus had dedicated a great new marble temple to Apollo on the Palatine in 28 B.C. into which the Sibylline books with the college of priests who looked after them had been transferred(the consultation of these at times of crisis was among the most sacred and mysterious of Roman religious rites). The 'festival days' for Apollo had been celebrated in Rome during July for hundreds of years.

74. **Do not commit your sayings to leaves:** this refers to the instructions given by Helenus at 3.441 ff.

79-80. **God who rode her...:** the imagery of a rider taming a horse is sustained here, and repeated in 100f.

85. **In Lavinium:** the name of the first Trojan settlement, from which they moved to Alba Longa and then to Rome; cf. 1.270ff.

88-90. **A Simois, a Xanthus...:** the Sibyl refers to the Trojan War against the Greeks, the like of which they will have to fight again. Simois and Xanthus were rivers of Troy, the scene of fierce fighting; the Italian equivalents will be the Tiber and its tributary the Numicius. The new Achilles will be Turnus, son of the nymph Venilia (Achilles was son of the goddess Thetis). In many ways Turnus is comparable with Achilles, as will be seen in the second half of the poem.

93. **Alien bride:** in the war against the Greeks this was Helen, in the new war it will be the princess Lavinia, daughter of King Latinus, who was betrothed to Turnus, but her father broke off the engagement (because of an oracle) and betrothed her to Aeneas

instead. This was the cause of the wars described in the second half of the poem.

97. **Greek city**: the city of Pallanteum, Evander's settlement on the future site of Rome, from which (as described in Book 8) Aeneas secured an alliance and armed help.

105. **I have forecast...**: this line is strongly reminiscent of the Stoic philosophy which taught its adherents to prepare themselves beforehand to face all possible calamities.

107. **Acheron**: like Cocytus (132), one of the rivers of the underworld, identified by Virgil with the Styx; it was thought to issue forth in Lake Avernus.

119. **Orpheus**: the legendary musician from Thrace; he was given permission to go down to the underworld to bring back his dead wife Eurydice.

121. **Pollux**: the twin of the mortal Castor who was permitted to share death with his brother, exchanging with him twice a year.

123. **Thesus and Hercules**: both of these went down to the underworld while alive, cf. 392 ff.

134. **Tartarus**: sometimes used generally for the underworld, as here, sometimes specifically the deepest dungeon of all (as in 551 ff.).

137. **Golden bough**: the magic talisman which gives entrance to the underworld. Sir James Frazer used it as the title of his great work on ancient folk-lore. Strangely we know nothing of the sources from which Virgil took it. It symbolises light in darkness, life in death; its mystery is enhanced by its comparison with the mistletoe (205 ff., where see note).

142. **Proserpine**: wife of Pluto (Dis), king of the underworld; the Greeks called her Persephone.

173. **Triton**: one of the sea-deities, famous for the music which he played on a sea-shell: cf. Wordsworth's 'or hear old Triton blow his wreathéd horn'.

193. **His mother's birds**: doves were sacred to Venus, Aeneas' mother.

201, **Foul-breathing**: the reference is to the sulphurous fumes of this area (cf. 240f.).

205–8. **Just as in depth of winter the mistletoe...**: the simile compares the strangeness of the golden bough on an ordinary tree with mistletoe which grows on host trees; it also deepens the sense of mystery because of the magic associations of mistletoe in ancient folk-lore.

235. **Misenum**: the conspicuously flat-topped hill just north of Naples still bears this name (cf. Cape Palinurus, 381).

242. **Avernus, the Birdless Place:** i.e. the Latin word *Avernus* is derived from the Greek negative prefix (the letter *a*) and *ornis*, a bird. This line is certainly spurious, a late addition to the text by a learned commentator in ancient times. The sulphurous fumes of this volcanic area account for the 'lethal miasma'.

264. **You gods . . .:** the new invocation heralds the beginning of the actual journey through the underworld, now that the preliminaries have all been completed.

265. **Chaos and Phlegethon:** Chaos is a primitive divinity (like Night and Earth in 250-1); Phlegethon is the burning river of Hades which encircles Tartarus itself (551).

273 ff. **Entrance way to Orcus . . .:** Orcus is another name for the underworld. The personification of abstract ideas (Grief, Anxiety etc.) was a well-known technique in Greek and Latin literature, but there is no evidence that they had previously been placed in the porch of Hell. Some of these shapes are specially relevant to Virgil's themes in the *Aeneid*, e.g. 'ever-haunting Anxiety' accompanies Aeneas through his encounters with the ghosts of Palinurus, Dido and Deiphobus; 'War, the bringer of Death', 'lunatic Strife' figure largely in the second half of the poem and reflect Virgil's personal experience during his youth of the Roman civil wars. Particular emphasis is put on strife by its position at the end of the list, and the horrifying line describing it. *line 281 whose viperous hair.....*

285. **Varieties of monsters:** these are fabulous creatures, animals or giants or composite images of both. The elimination of the Hydra and of Geryon were two of Hercules' twelve labours.

299. **Charon:** the ferryman of the dead was a traditional figure in the geography of the underworld; he was frequently depicted on tombstones and a coin was often buried with the dead body to pay the fare.

309-12. **Multitudinous as the leaves . . .:** a famous simile imitated by Milton 'Thick as autumnal leaves that strow the brooks in Vallombrosa . . .' (P.L. 1.302f.). The point of comparison is firstly the number, secondly the fluttering, thirdly the end of a period (the summer of the leaves and the birds, the worldly life of the ghosts).

324. **Even the gods . . .:** to swear by the River Styx was the most sacred oath possible.

329. **A hundred years:** i.e. after this period the ghost was allowed to cross the Styx. Other versions made the period a thousand years, or perpetual.

333. **Death's fulfilment:** i.e. burial.

334-6. **Leucaspis and Orontes . . .:** the reference is to the storm at 1.113 ff. where Orontes' ship with its Lycians was sunk before Aeneas' eyes. Leucaspis who was also on this ship was not mentioned there.

337.   **Palinurus:**   the story of how he was thrown overboard by the god Sleep was told in 5.833 ff.

346.   **Unharmed by sea:**   this oracular promise by Phoebus Apollo is not mentioned elsewhere. Palinurus' explanation shows that he did in fact complete the sea-voyage: he reached land but was then murdered.

366.   **Velia:**   south of Naples, near Cape Palinurus (381) where Palinurus reached Italy.

376.   **Give up this hope . . .:**   these are hard and chilling words, typical of the atmosphere of gloom and sorrow in the underworld all the way to Elysium where suddenly the radiant light of hope breaks through.

392-7.   **Not with impunity . . .:**   Charon refers to how on a previous occasion he stretched a point and ferried living people across: an ancient commentator tells us that he was punished by a year's imprisonment for this breach of the conditions of his employment. One of Hercules' labours was to bring back from the underworld the watch-dog Cerberus; Theseus and Pirithous went down to rescue Proserpine, Pluto's queen whom he had abducted while she was gathering flowers with her mother Demeter, sister of Jupiter and Pluto (hence 'uncle', 402).

413.   **Ramshackle craft:**   this touch of humour rounds off an interlude which has relieved the tension after the emotional confrontation with Palinurus.

426-547.   **At once were voices heard . . .:**   the area which Aeneas now enters may be called Limbo: it is the neutral area, not for the blessed nor for the great sinners. In it reside (apparently for ever – the impression given is a very static one) those whose lives ended untimely: babies, the unjustly condemned, suicides, those who died for unhappy love, those killed in war. It is not profitable to question the theological relationship of this section with the later explanation given by Anchises (724ff.) of life after death: Limbo, a sad and hopeless place, serves Virgil's poetic purposes at this stage in the narrative, especially in providing a setting for the tragic ghosts of Aeneas' past, Dido and Deiphobus.

432.   **Minos:**   one of the traditional judges of the underworld; others were Rhadamanthus (566) and Aeacus.

441.   **The vale of mourning:**   the *Lugentes Campi* ('sorrowing fields'), a memorable phrase apparently invented by Virgil.

445-9.   **Here Aeneas descried . . .:**   this is a 'crowd scene' of seven famous heroines, presented rapidly, and in such a way that we have no time to sorrow over their fate. None has figured (except for a mention of Pasiphae) in the *Aeneid*, and our sympathies are not engaged. But at the mention of the eighth heroine, Phoenician Dido, we are returned to the personal involvement which Virgil sought from us throughout her story, a story which had played so large a part in the poem. For mythological details of these seven heroines see the glossary; for a detailed literary analysis of 445–76 see Appendix 3.

460.   **Not of my own will:**   this was the point which Aeneas had constantly tried to make to Dido in her lifetime. She is as unable to accept it now as she had been then.

469.   **She would not turn to him:**   the narrative recalls the ghost of Ajax rejecting Odysseus in Homer's *Odyssey* (11.543 ff.), 'a silence', as Longinus says, 'more sublime than any words'.

473.   **Sychaeus:**   the story of his murder was told at 1.343 ff.

479–80.   **Here Tydeus ... Adrastus:**   three of the leaders in the legendary war of the 'Seven against Thebes'. Notice how here again Virgil first uses a crowd scene before focussing the attention on the central figure, Deiphobus.

483–5.   **Glaucus ... Idaeus:**   Trojans who fell in the war against the Greeks, all known to Aeneas.

494.   **Deiphobus:**   a son of Priam, one of Troy's champions. He was briefly mentioned in Book 2, and here he symbolises all those who fell on Troy's last night, when Aeneas escaped. Aeneas' feelings of guilt over this fact are evident throughout the passage: it is the wretched phantom of Deiphobus who speaks words of encouragement to Aeneas, and not vice versa.

511–2.   **Lacaenian woman:**   Helen of Sparta (Lacedaemon).

515.   **Horse of doom:**   the story of Troy's capture through the Greek device of the wooden horse was told in Book 2.

519.   **Signalled the Greeks from our citadel:**   a clearer translation would be 'from our citadel signalled the Greeks'. Helen is on the citadel leading the dance in honour of Bacchus and sends a fire-signal to the Greek fleet to indicate that the wooden horse is inside and that they should land and advance to be let in. The tradition of this part of the legend varied very much – in some versions it was Sinon who sent the signal, and in Book 2 Virgil's description of Helen hiding at the temple of Vesta at this time seems to conflict with the version here.

523.   **Nonpareil wife:**   highly sarcastic. Deiphobus had married Helen after the death of Paris towards the end of the Trojan War.

526.   **Lover:**   a very biased word for Deiphobus to use of Menelaus, her real husband.

546. **With better luck than mine**: the Latin is more ambiguous ('enjoy happier fates'), and implies not only happier than Deiphobus himself has had, but happier than Aeneas has had so far. These last words of Deiphobus mark the turning-point for Aeneas – from now on he concentrates his attention on the happier fates that lie ahead rather than the unhappiness of the past.

549 ff. **Overhanging a spread of battlements...**: the description of Tartarus, deepest dungeon of the greatest sinners, is a brilliantly portrayed transition piece between the end of Aeneas' encounters with ghosts of his past and his arrival in Elysium to meet his father. The sinners named are from mythological tradition (mostly from Homer), but Virgil adds categories of unnamed sinners whose sins are more relevant to his own times (608 ff., 621 ff.).

582. **Twin sons of Aloeus**: Otus and Ephialtes, who took part in the rebellion of the Giants and Titans against Jupiter, and by piling mountains on top of each other (Pelion on Ossa) tried to invade heaven.

595. **Tityos**: a giant (full nine acres) who assaulted the goddess Latona: his punishment is like that of Prometheus.

601-7. **The Lapithae, Ixion or Pirithous...**: the Lapiths were a legendary Thessalian people, best known for their battle against the Centaurs, depicted on the Parthenon. The normal version of Ixion's fate (he assaulted Juno) is that he was stretched out on a wheel (616-7), and Pirithous was generally chained: the punishment assigned to them here is that of Tantalus, starving in sight of plenty (hence our word tantalise). Either the text has been corrupted or (as is more likely) Virgil has varied the legend.

608-13. **Here are those ...**: these are categories of sinners specially appropriate to Roman life, which valued very highly the sanctity of family ties, and the keeping of faith. Cf. also 620-4.

638. **Happy Place**: this is Elysium, home of the blessed, where Anchises awaits them. The Islands of the Blessed occur as early as Homer, but they are only for the sons of gods: Virgil's Elysium (see note on 660-4) is open to all who have deserved to go there because of a life well-lived on earth.

645. **Orpheus**: the mythological founder of music, also of significance here because of the religious ideas associated with his name which Anchises expounds in 724 ff.

648-50. **Teucer... Dardanus**: all these were ancestors of the Trojans.

659. **Eridanus**: the River Po, the main river of Virgil's own countryside; here it is said to originate in Elysium.

660-4. **Here were assembled ...**: these categories of the

virtuous match and contrast with the categories of sinners in Tartarus (608–13). Notice how the last category of all ('men whose kindness to other people...') is by far the widest, and opens the gates of Elysium to all mankind.

667. **Musaeus:** like Orpheus, a legendary musician.

694. **How I dreaded...:** Anchises refers to Aeneas' stay with Dido in Carthage (Book 4), when he had to be reminded by Jupiter that he must leave her in order to fulfil his mission.

695. **Your image:** Anchises had appeared in dreams to Aeneas at Carthage (4.351ff.), and again in Sicily (5.722f.), on this last occasion instructing Aeneas to visit him in the underworld.

724 ff. **First, you must know...:** Anchises' speech gives a view of this world and the after-life which is the direct opposite of Homer's. In the Homeric world this life was the important one, and the life after death a miserable wraith-like existence: here we are told that this life is merely a preparation for a fuller and richer life hereafter. This religious belief is based on ideas which first arose in the Greek mystery religions (such as Orphism and Pythagoreanism) in the sixth century B.C.: they were deepened and purified by Plato, and many aspects of this (though not the transmigration of souls) passed into Roman Stoicism.

743 ff. **Each of us finds in the next world ...:** the doctrine which Virgil is here putting forward is that after purification all souls pass through Elysium and a few of the purest (such as Anchises) stay there before finally being re-united with God whence they came. All the others are born again to try to live a better life.

749. **Lethe:** the river gets its name from the Greek word meaning 'forgetfulness'.

756–853. **Listen, for I will show you ...:** Anchises' long speech, in which he surveys the ghosts of future Roman heroes waiting to be born, is one of the most directly patriotic passages in the poem. It falls into two sections: the first (to 805) describes the early kings of Alba, then Romulus and Augustus, and is separated from the second section by the interposed question 'Do we still hesitate then ...?' Aeneas does not reply, but the reader is confident that now that Aeneas realises how much depends on him, there can be no more hesitation. The second half describes the Roman kings and many heroes of the Republic, ending with a memorable summary of Rome's mission (see note on 847–53).

772. **The oak leaves:** the 'civic crown' of oak leaves was awarded to Romans who had saved the life of a fellow-citizen in battle. It had been voted to Augustus as a perpetual honour in 27 B.C., and adorned the doors of his palace.

778. **Romulus:** the first king of Rome is descended both from Trojan ancestry (the stock of Assaracus) by his mother Ilia (also called Rhea Silvia) and from Italian ancestry by the Italian god of war, Mars.

784. **Cybele:** the Great Mother (*Magna Mater*) of the gods. Rome is compared with her as being similarly 'blessed in her breed', and there is also a pictorial comparison between the 'turreted crown' which Cybele wore and the turrets of the circular wall round the seven hills of Rome. 820

789. **Caesar:** this means Augustus Caesar (not Julius Caesar who is referred to later, 826 ff.). Consequently a clearer translation of 791 would be 'Yes, here, here is the man . . .'.

792. **Caesar Augustus, son of a god:** he was descended through Ascanius (whose other name was Iulus – hence Julius, the name Augustus took when adopted by Julius Caesar) from Aeneas and therefore Venus; but the more immediate reference is to the deification after death of his adoptive father Julius Caesar.

794. **Age of gold:** the idea of a return by the Romans to the legendary Golden Age when Saturnus was king of the gods (cf. 8.319 ff.) is powerfully expressed in the fourth *Eclogue*. The concept of an idyllic Golden Age in the mythical past was frequent in Greek and Latin literature, but Virgil is the first to suggest that a return to it was about to take place.

798–800. **Caspian realm . . . seven mouths of the Nile:** the Caspian and the Crimean are mentioned (like the Garamants and Indians, 794) as examples of people at the very boundaries of the known world. The Nile however has special significance: it refers to the final victory by Augustus at Actium in 31 B.C. over Antony and Cleopatra, queen of Egypt (see 8.675 ff.).

801–5. **Hercules . . . Bacchus . . .:** the comparison with these two indicates firstly (as Virgil says) that Augustus, like them, will extend his influence over the whole world; secondly that like them he will make possible a civilised way of life (as Hercules did with his twelve labours and Bacchus by taming wild nature, here symbolised by tigers); thirdly that like them he is a mortal who will be deified.

805. **Mount Nysa:** the name of a mountain in Asia Minor where Bacchus' worship was supposed to have originated, but subsequently given to mountains in various parts of the world with which Bacchus was especially associated.

806. **Do we still hesitate . . .?:** see note on 756–853.

810. **Cures:** a little town in Sabine territory from which Numa Pompilius, the second king of Rome, came. Numa was especially

associated with religious rites and peaceful law-giving, in contrast with Romulus, a king of warlike qualities.

817. **The Tarquin kings:** Tarquin the elder was fifth king of Rome (Tullus and Ancus, just mentioned, were third and fourth); Tarquin the Proud was the seventh and last king. The sixth king, Servius Tullius, is not mentioned in order that the Tarquins can be dealt with together. Tarquin the Proud was expelled by Brutus following the rape of Lucretia by Tarquin's son Sextus, and a republic was set up in which Brutus became one of the first consuls (509 B.C.). It is strange that Virgil should call Brutus 'arrogant as they': just possibly there is an undertone of reference to the conspirator Marcus Brutus who took part in the assassination of Julius Caesar in 44 B.C.

820-2. **When his sons...:** Tarquin endeavoured to return to Rome, with the help of Lars Porsenna of Clusium, and Brutus' sons joined him. Their father therefore had the tragic task of executing them for treason. The story was used by other writers as an illustration of the splendid devotion to duty of the true Roman, but Virgil presents it in its aspect of pathos.

824 ff. **The Decii, the Drusi, Torquatus...:** for these Roman heroes, and others mentioned in the rest of the speech, see the Glossary.

826. **Those twin souls:** Caesar and Pompey, the leaders of the civil war which began in 49 B.C. when Caesar marched on Italy from Gaul ('Alpine strongholds') and finally defeated Pompey whose army had largely been recruited in the East. Because Caesar was descended from Anchises (see note on 792) he is specially appealed to (834-5).

836. **That one:** Memmius, who celebrated a triumph for his conquest of the Greek city Corinth in 146 B.C.

838. **That one:** Aemilius Paulus, who defeated King Perses of Macedonia in 168 B.C.: Perses claimed descent from Achilles, and thus Aeacus (Achilles' grandfather). These Roman victories over the Greeks are put in terms appropriate to Aeneas' own times ('Argos and Agamemnon's Mycenae').

840. **Sacrilege done to Minerva:** the rape of Cassandra by Ajax, son of Oileus, in Minerva's temple.

845. **Fabius:** this is Fabius Maximus who gained the cognomen Cunctator ('Delayer') because he saved Rome in her darkest hour, after severe defeats by Hannibal in 217 and 216 B.C., by delaying tactics, gradually restoring the shattered strength of the Romans and wearing the invading Hannibal down. Fabius is accorded the place of honour at the end of the pageant because he

exorcises Dido's plea for vengeance (4.625 ff.): Hannibal was her avenger, but Fabius managed to survive against him.

847–53. **Let others fashion ...**: this is perhaps the clearest statement in the whole poem of the nature of Rome's mission. The 'others' referred to are, of course, the Greeks: Anchises concedes to them greater excellence in sculpture (as he was bound to), in oratory (rather surprising this in view of the achievements of Cicero) and in astronomy (certainly in the pure sciences the Greeks, especially the Alexandrian Greeks, were pre-eminent). The Roman claim to excel in government was fully justified: the stability and peace of the Roman empire (notwithstanding all its faults) was unmatched by any other ancient people and led to the preservation of the Greco-Roman heritage of which European civilisation is the heir.

852. **Be this your art**: as opposed to the 'fine arts' of the Greeks.

To practise men in the habit of peace: the translation here accepts a wrong reading (*pacisque imponere morem*). The true reading is *pacique*: the translation might be 'to crown peace with civilisation'. First, as a foundation, the Romans establish peace (by means of military conquest), and on that foundation they build the civilised way of life which they had developed, and which other European peoples at the time (like the Britons, the Gauls and the Germans) did not possess.

855. **Marcellus**: a leading Roman general of the period of the Second Punic War against Carthage, just before which the Gauls of Northern Italy had rebelled against Roman rule.

859. **Give to Quirinus**: he was awarded the special mark of honour known as the *spolia opima*, given for killing the enemy general in battle. Before him only Romulus and Cossus (841) had won this distinction. He dedicates them to the Roman god Quirinus.

861. **A youth of fine appearance**: this is the young Marcellus (finally named in 883) who was marked out as Augustus' heir but died in his teens in 23 B.C. Notice how the triumphant pageant is concluded with this contrasting picture of tragedy. It is Virgil's way to juxtapose the opposing experiences of mankind: joy and sorrow, triumph and disaster.

872. **Campus Martius**: an open space by the Tiber where Marcellus' funeral was held.

889. **And fired his heart ...**: this summarises the effect upon Aeneas of the vision of his future – there will be no further hesitation, but he will continue with the utmost resolution to try to bring to pass the great future of Rome.

891.   **Laurentines ... Latinus:**   the Laurentines were the inhabitants of Latium, ruled by King Latinus, against whom in the end Aeneas had to wage war (as is told in the second half of the *Aeneid*).

893.   **Two gates of Sleep:**   the imagery is taken from Homer and adapted by Virgil as a way of exit from the underworld. Much has been written about why Aeneas departs by the gate of false dreams. At the simplest it can be said that Aeneas is not a 'genuine apparition' (not an apparition at all, in fact) and therefore is disqualified from going out through the gate of horn. But most readers will feel that Virgil wishes to indicate more than this – perhaps that his whole description of the underworld has been a personal poetic vision, a dream or a fantasy which must be taken on those terms. 'We are such stuff as dreams are made on.'

Book seven

The seventh book begins the movement of the second half of the poem: the voyages are over, Aeneas arrives at the Tiber, and in a new invocation Virgil speaks of his 'grander theme'. The theme is the foundation of Aeneas' city in the face of violent opposition, inspired by Juno in Turnus, and the problem which Virgil explores is how this opposition can best be confronted, whether by gentleness, negotiation, or force, or a variation between these possibilities according to each particular situation.

The book divides naturally into three sections. The first part (1–285) is serene and happy, as the Trojans are well received by King Latinus, and his daughter Lavinia is betrothed to Aeneas, in fulfilment of an oracle. But this happy situation is shattered by the intervention (at 286) of Juno, even more savagely resentful now than at the beginning of the poem; she summons the fiend Allecto from the underworld to breathe frenzy and fury into Queen Amata and Turnus. Both of these are very ready to be inflamed; the symbolic relationship of divine powers to human qualities is here seen very clearly. War breaks out and the final section of the book (641 ff.) is taken up with a catalogue of the Italian forces. It was unexpected that this traditional piece of epic technique (going back to the catalogue of the Greek ships in *Iliad* 2) should be devoted to the enemy forces; but by this means Virgil is able to portray his own deep love for the peoples and places of his native land, and prepare the reader for the sympathetic treatment of the Italians in the books which follow, and in particular for the final reconciliation of Juno in Book 12 when she obtains peace conditions very much more favourable to the Italians than to the Trojans. After all, the Romans were much more Italian than Trojan.

1. **Caieta:** for this aetiological association of the past with the present through place names cf. Misenus and Palinurus in Book 6. The modern name of this town, some fifty miles north of Cumae from which the Trojans have just sailed, is Gaeta.

10. **Circe's land:** the enchantress Circe, who by her spells turned humans into animals (especially pigs) was well-known in mythology from Homer's time onwards (*Odyssey* 10.221 ff.). By Virgil's time her island (located half-way between Naples and the mouth of the Tiber) had become a promontory, as it is now (Monte Circeo). Cf. Milton, *Comus* 50 ff.:

> Who knows not Circe,
> The daughter of the Sun? whose charmèd cup
> Whoever tasted, lost his upright shape,
> And downward fell into a groveling swine.

23-4. **Neptune ... got them away:** this is Aeneas' last encounter with the world of the *Odyssey*; cf. the Harpies, Scylla and Charybdis, and the Cyclops in Book 3 and the Sirens in Book 5.

25 ff. **Now was the sea's face...:** Aeneas arrives at the Tiber at long last, and Virgil gives an idyllic picture of dawn, calm weather and bird song to mark his journey's end.

37-45. **Come, Muse of Love ...:** this new invocation marks the transition in the poem from Aeneas' voyage, now completed, to the war which he had to fight before he could found his city. The invocation to the Muse of Love suggests that the *casus belli* was the princess Lavinia, wooed by Turnus but soon to be promised to Aeneas in fulfilment of an oracle (96 ff., 255 ff.). The 'levies of the Etruscans' refers to the aid sent by Evander (Book 8) to the Trojans.

44-5. **A grander train...:** it is interesting that Virgil evidently regarded the second half of his poem as more important than the first: readers of the *Aeneid* ever since it was published have generally preferred the first half. Among possible reasons for Virgil's statement could be: (i) after the preliminaries he now comes to the fulfilment of Aeneas' mission; (ii) the setting is no longer Greece or Africa or Sicily but Virgil's own Italy; (iii) the ancient world always regarded battle poetry as the highest type – the *Iliad* was greatly preferred to the *Odyssey*; (iv) Virgil's deepest problem is constantly presented in the books to follow, namely the problem of how to confront violent opposition. This he explored in countless situations, showing how Aeneas would much prefer peace but is driven to war, and often fights it savagely.

47-8. Faunus ... Marica: these were traditional Italian deities.

49. Saturn: the king of heaven before Jupiter; thus the native Italians are given the highest possible dignity and lineage, and also associated with the legendary Golden Age under Saturn (cf. 8.319ff.).

52. One daughter: i.e. Lavinia (71).

116. We're eating our tables too: this is a fulfilment of the prophecy of the Harpy Celaeno (3.250ff.). Aeneas is mistaken in attributing it to Anchises (123); this mistake is perhaps a reflection of the very large part played by Anchises in guiding and advising Aeneas on his voyage.

139. Juppiter, patron of Ida ...: the reference is to Jupiter's birth on Mt Ida in Crete which gave its name to the Trojan Mt Ida. The Phrygian Mother is Cybele, Great Mother of the Gods, especially associated with Mt Berecynthus in Phrygia near Troy.

151. Numicius: a small tributary of the Tiber.

189-90. Picus ... Circe: Picus has accoutrements ('augur's staff', 'toga purple-striped', 'holy shield') which anticipate the ceremonial objects of the Romans. The scene suddenly and strangely shifts from antiquarian history to the magic mythology of the metamorphosis of Picus, when he spurned Circe, into a woodpecker (a story told at length by Ovid, *Met.* 14.320ff.).

206. Dardanus: Latinus refers to the Italian origin of Dardanus, founder of Troy, now deified; cf. 3.167-8.

209. Corythus: Dardanus' mortal father (his immortal father was Jupiter, 220); an Italian city in Etruria ('Tuscan') was called after him (3.170).

222. Unleashed from cruel Mycenae: the storm is a metaphor for the Greek invasion, led by Agamemnon, king of Mycenae.

286ff. But look ...: the sudden transition from peace and serenity is motivated by Juno, returning from her beloved Argos, one of the leading cities of Greece once ruled by Inachus. Her angry and sarcastic speech and her subsequent actions balance her intervention in Book 1, when she shipwrecked the Trojans: here her intentions are more formidable still, as she proceeds to enlist the aid of the fiends of Hell.

302. The Syrtes, Scylla ...: Juno refers to the storm she aroused in Book 1 when the Trojans were driven to Carthage through the treacherous waters known as the Syrtes, and to the mythological creatures guarding the Straits of Messina, which the Trojans managed to avoid (3.558ff.).

304-6.   **Mars ... Calydon:**   as at 1.39 ff. Juno gives examples of other gods who were permitted to destroy their enemies: Mars, insulted by the Lapiths, a people of northern Greece, caused the Centaurs to fight them; Diana was slighted by the king of Calydon and sent a wild boar to ravage the land.

315-16.   **What I can do is to postpone ...:**   this is the essence of Juno's position: she cannot change Fate, but she can postpone it, make its fulfilment more difficult, perhaps even less effective.

319.   **Not only Hecuba:**   the mother of Paris (321), who caused the Greco-Trojan war by carrying off Helen. Similarly Aeneas will cause a war with the Italians by wishing to marry Lavinia.

325.   **Allecto:**   one of the Furies of Hell, sister of Tisiphone (6.555) and Megaera (12.846). She symbolises qualities of hatred and wild frenzy.

344 ff.   **The queen ...:**   Amata is in a mood ready to receive the Fury; she already has in her the sparks of violent and passionate resentment (over the slight to her favourite Turnus) which Allecto can fan to flame. The description of how Allecto does so, by means of the snake, is daemonic and terrifying.

363-4.   **It's Paris all over again ...:**   the reference is to the well-known incident which started the Trojan war, when Paris abducted Helen, daughter of Jupiter and Leda, from her husband Menelaus of Sparta.

371-2.   **Now Turnus ...:**   Amata means that Turnus, who is not in any case a Latin but a Rutulian, comes from a city (Ardea) founded by the Greek Danae, daughter of Acrisius (410). Inachus was the legendary founder of Argos, which with Mycenae was Greece's chief town at this time.

378 ff.   **A top goes spinning ...:**   this is a very remarkable simile; Virgil (unlike Homer) does not generally use similes drawn from everyday life. Here the point of comparison is not merely the wild speed of Amata's movements, but also the fact that she has become, as it were, the plaything of Allecto.

385.   **The call of Bacchus:**   the other reference to the wild worship of Bacchus by his female devotees is in an equally threatening passage, describing the madness of Dido (4.300 ff.).

390.   **Thyrsus:**   a wand used by the devotees of Bacchus.

410.   **Danae ...:**   see note on 371-2.

425-6.   **Go then ...:**   Allecto (disguised as Calybe) refers to the services already performed by Turnus for the Latins in their wars against the Tuscans.

435-6.   **Deriding her prophecy:**   this first appearance of Turnus in the poem shows him to be impetuous and self-confident even before he is fired to passionate anger by Allecto's burning brand. He is the kind of man in whom Juno and Allecto can stir up the passions and hatreds which they plan.

483 ff.   **There was a stag...:**   this episode, which sparked off the war, is described with an emotional depth of pathos approximating to the mood of lyric or elegiac poetry.

516–17.   **The lake of Diana ... Velinus:**   localities near the Tiber, well-known in Virgil's time.

559.   **Away, then!:**   even Juno, responsible for so much of the suffering in the poem, is sickened by Allecto's blood-lust.

565.   **The Vale of Amsanctus:**   a valley with a sulphurous lake in Campania, fabled – like Avernus – to be an entrance to the underworld.

600.   **But shutting himself in his palace:**   the old King Latinus, peaceful and in the end ineffective, is a complete contrast to the violent and energetic Turnus.

601.   **There was a custom:**   this refers to the opening of the gates of war (607).

604–6.   **Getae ... Parthians:**   all peoples on the frontiers of Rome's empire; the Parthians in particular were formidable enemies, having captured Roman standards at the battle of Carrhae in 53 B.C.   Augustus eventually recovered them.

607.   **Twin gates of War:**   in the temple of Janus (610); they were open (indicating that Rome was at war) through most of Rome's history, but were twice closed by Augustus (in 29 and 25 B.C.).

612–13.   **Quirinal ... cincture:**   the ceremonial attire of the chief magistrate when he declared war.

635–6.   **To this has come...:**   this kind of lamentation over the destruction of peaceful agricultural pursuits by the requirements of war is reminiscent of the *Georgics*, written during the final period of Rome's civil wars.

641 ff.   **Muses, throw Helicon wide now! ...:**   the new invocation introduces a catalogue of Italian forces. See introductory note to this Book.

647.   **Mezentius:**   the first enemy general contrasts very much with Aeneas, in his 'irreligious' attitude: the horrifying behaviour which caused him to be exiled by the Tuscans is told at 8.483 ff, and his death is described at the end of Book 10.

649.   **Lausus:**   a very sympathetic figure; his death at the hands of Aeneas (10.810 ff) is told with great pathos.

656.   **Aventinus:**   he does not figure again in the poem. He is connected with the Aventine Hill (659), one of the seven hills of Rome.

661-3. **Hercules...**: according to one version of the legend, he was born at Tiryns, in southern Greece. The reference to Geryon anticipates the story of Hercules and Cacus (8.190ff.), as it was on his way back from killing the Spanish ('Iberian') giant Geryon that Hercules passed through Latium and killed Cacus.

672. **Catillus and mettlesome Coras**: these twins from Tibur (modern Tivoli, a few miles east of Rome) are briefly mentioned again in the fighting in Book 11.

678. **Caeculus**: the founder of Praeneste, one of the most famous towns of Latium, is mentioned briefly again in Book 10. Virgil puts the emphasis here, as in the subsequent descriptions, on the peoples and the places of his native Italy rather than on the generals themselves. The place-names of 682-5 are all localities near Rome.

691. **Messapus**: he figures much more in the poem, as one of Turnus' strongest supporters, than most of the other generals of this catalogue. The place-names (695-7) again are all local.

701. **Cayster**: a river in Asia famous for its swans.

706-9. **Clausus...**: he has a brief mention again in Book 10. The Sabines and the Romans united under the second king of Rome, a Sabine himself, Numa Pompilius. The 'Claudian clan' was of course one of the most famous of Roman families.

710-17. **Amiternian ... Allia**: again the place-names are all local; Virgil makes great play with the associations they would carry with Roman readers.

717. **Allia (ill-omened name!)**: this local river was the scene of one of Rome's worst military disasters, when they were defeated by the Gauls in 390 B.C. The anniversary of the battle was considered an ill-omened day throughout Roman history.

723. **Halaesus**: a Greek associated with the territory rather further south, in Campania. He is mentioned again in Book 10.

733. **Oebalus**: his territory is a little further south still, around the region of Naples. He is not mentioned again in the poem.

744. **Ufens**: he comes from the east of Rome; the toughness of his followers is reflected in the speech of the Italian Numanus (9.603ff). He is mentioned again in Books 8, 10 and 12.

752. **Umbro**: Virgil here varies his list by this glimpse of the almost supernatural skill of Umbro, which however did not avail him in war. His territory was east of Rome, where Marruvium, Angitia and Fucinus were situated.

762ff. **Virbius...**: again Virgil varies his list, this time with a sustained and elaborate piece of mythology, by introducing a son of Hippolytus, whom the Romans identified with their deity Virbius.

Aricia was a deity of the Arician grove near Alba Longa, Egeria a nymph, Diana's shrine (at Nemi) a very famous one. The Greek story tells of how Theseus' wife Phaedra fell in love with her stepson Hippolytus, and when he refused her she committed suicide and left a note accusing Hippolytus. At Theseus' request Nepture caused Hippolytus' horses to be frightened by a sea-monster, and Hippolytus was killed. The story is the subject of Euripides' play *Hippolytus*. The sequel (Hippolytus' restoration to life) is told by Ovid (*Met.* I5.497 ff.).

785. **A Chimaera:** this emblem which Turnus wears suggests archaic violence and love of fighting.

790-2. **Io, now changed to a heifer:** the story is told by Ovid in *Met.* 1.583 ff. of how Juno persecuted Io, daughter of the Argive river-god Inachus, because Jupiter was her lover, and changed her into a cow, guarded by the hundred-eyed Argus. The significance of this emblem may be to represent the power of Juno for evil.

793 ff. **At Turnus' heels ...:** these peoples are from places around the Rutulian territory from which Turnus came, to the south of the Tiber.

803 ff. **Camilla ...:** the warrior-maiden (whose exploits and death are recounted in Book 11) is a strange mixture of 'facing the horrors of battle' and of the pastoral, supernatural world ('skimmed along the blades', 'flitted over the waves'). This mixture is symbolised in the last line: country myrtle is appropriate for the gentle quasi-magical pastoral world (the Latin word here rendered by 'country' is in fact *pastoralis*), but it is tipped with a warhead.

Book eight

This book tells of the visit of Aeneas to Evander, and is filled with peaceful and serene scenes, a marked contrast with the first outbreak of war in Book 7 and the full-scale descriptions of battle in Books 9-12. Its first part describes Aeneas' voyage up the Tiber to Evander's city on the site of future Rome; it is idyllic and gentle as the two leaders form their alliance. The undertones of impending disaster and violence make this brief interlude all the more poignant.

This is the most Roman book of all: set as it is on the seven hills it provides an opportunity for Virgil to write of the famous landmarks of Rome which Evander shows to Aeneas, and in addition the description of the pictures on Aeneas' shield forms a sustained patriotic preview of Rome's greatness comparable with the pageant of Roman heroes which concluded Book 6. For a discussion of the pictures on the shield see note on 626ff. A very full and sympathetic account of the literary characteristics of this book is given in K.W. Gransden's edition (Cambridge, 1976).

9. **Diomedes:** the Greek warrior had settled in southern Italy after the Trojan War; the negative result of this embassy is described at 11.225ff.

44-6. **A great white sow...:** these verses are repeated from the prophecy of Helenus in 3.390ff., where see the note. The prophecy is fulfilled at 81ff.

54. **Pallanteum:** Evander's settlement on the site of future Rome is called after an Arcadian ancestor Pallas; Evander's son, who figures largely in the narrative to come, had the same name.

64. **Caerulean:** the colour of bright water.

77. **Horned River:** river-gods were often depicted by the Romans with bull-like faces.

103. **Hercules, heir of Amphitryon:** Hercules was really son of Jupiter, but Amphitryon was his mortal father.

132. **The kinship between our fathers:** this is explained in the lines which follow.

146. **Daunian:** Turnus' father was Daunus, king of part of Apulia in southern Italy.

158. **Hesione:** Hesione was married to Telamon who lived in the Greek island of Salamis; evidently Priam and Anchises passed through Arcadia on the occasion of their visit to Hesione.

165. **Pheneus:** a town in Arcadia.

203. **Triform Geryon:** it was one of Hercules' twelve labours to kill the three-bodied Spanish giant Geryon and drive away his cattle.

219. **Son of Alcides:** Hercules was the grandson of Alceus.

269–72. **Potitius ... Pinarian family ... Ara Maxima:** the annual ceremony in honour of Hercules took place at the Ara Maxima, and was associated with the Potitii and the Pinarii as its founders.

285. **The Salii:** a famous Roman college of priests.

291. **Troy and Oechalia:** Hercules destroyed Troy to take vengeance on Laomedon (2.643), and Oechalia (in Euboea) when its king refused him the promised marriage with his daughter.

291 ff. **Stepmother, hostile Juno ...:** she was hostile to Hercules because he was the son of Jupiter and Alcmena; she forced him to serve king Eurystheus of Mycenae and perform his twelve labours, several of which are listed in the lines that follow.

323. **Latium – a word...:** the Latin word for 'taking refuge' is *latere*. Saturn was driven from the kingship of heaven by his son Jupiter: the mythological Golden Age of the past was always associated with him, and Italy was often called the land of Saturn (329).

338. **Carmental gate:** this was a well-known gate of Rome in Virgil's time, near the Tiber. The places which are described in the following lines were all famous landmarks in Rome.

343. **Lupercal:** Pan was a rural god of Arcadia; his Greek epithet Lycaean means 'connected with wolves'; *lupus* is the Latin word for wolf.

345. **Argiletum:** the potters' quarter in Rome, here derived by Virgil from Argos, a one-time friend of Evander, and *letum* ('death').

347. **Tarpeian site:** a famous cliff on the Capitol hill.

361. **The Forum ... the elegant Ship-Place:** the Forum was the business centre of Rome, the Ship-Place (Carinae) a fashionable suburb.

374-5. **Argive... Pergamum:** Venus refers to the Greek attack on Troy; she was a strong supporter of Troy.

384. **Thetis... Tithonus:** at the request of the sea-deity Thetis, Vulcan (Hephaestus) made new armour for her son Achilles. This is described in Homer, *Iliad* 18. The wife of Tithonus was the dawn-goddess Aurora; Vulcan made armour for her son Memnon.

416. **Aeolian Lipare:** the island of Aeolus, god of the winds (Homer, *Odyssey* 10.1 ff.).

419. **The Cyclops' fires:** they were generally located beneath Mt. Etna (3.569 ff.); here the version is that their island Vulcania (modern Vulcano, in the Lipari islands) was connected by underground caves with Etna. Virgil seems to have enjoyed writing this high-flown and baroque descriptive piece.

454. **The lord of Lemnos:** the island of Lemnos, in the Aegean Sea, was Vulcan's favourite haunt.

459. **Tegea:** his original home in southern Greece.

478-9. **Caere... Lydia:** there was a well-established tradition that the Etruscans had come from Asia Minor; cf. 2.781.

505. **Tarchon:** leader of the Etruscans, said to have been the founder of the town Tarquinii.

538-40. **How many shields...:** these words are very similar to those used in 1.100f. about the Trojan War; now that slaughter must be repeated.

560 ff. **If Jupiter would only restore ...:** Evander's nostalgic speech is reminiscent of Nestor's speeches in the *Iliad* (7.132 ff., 11.670 ff.). The story of how Evander killed the triple-bodied Erulus (a doublet of Geryon) at Praeneste (cf. 7.678) is known only from this passage.

572 ff. **Ye heaven-dwellers...:** the pathos of Evander's prayer is very strong as Virgil begins to concentrate our attention on Pallas whose death at Turnus' hands motivates Aeneas' final act of anger and vengeance. Compare with this passage Evander's speech at 11.152 ff.

602. **Silvanus:** an ancient Roman rural deity, not unlike the Greek Pan.

626 ff. **Upon this shield ...:** the rest of this book is taken up with the description of pictures wrought on the shield which Vulcan has made. It recalls the description in Homer, *Iliad* 18. 478 ff., of the shield made by Hephaestus (the Greek fire-god) for Achilles; but both the motivation for the episode and the nature of the pictures are

entirely different. The motivation in Homer is logically extremely clear. Achilles had lent his armour to Patroclus, whom Hector had killed and stripped, so that Achilles needs new armour. In Virgil Aeneas has no such immediate need of armour, but the episode offers Virgil the opportunity of indicating by means of the pictures, just before the full-scale fighting begins, what is to be achieved by it. With the memory of these famous future scenes from Roman history Aeneas can more easily bear the suffering and bloodshed of the war which he must fight in order to bring them to pass.

The description in Homer of the pictures on Achilles' shield is a general one of aspects of Greek life, of a city at peace, a city at war, ploughing, reaping, dancing; Virgil's pictures are of specific historical scenes of Rome's future history. They are chosen partly for their visual impact, partly as being critical moments, but largely because they illustrate typical Roman virtues such as keeping faith, worshipping the gods, bravery in adversity and finally the triumph of Roman values over those of the East at the battle of Actium.

The pattern of the pictures is clear: in the centre are three scenes of the battle of Actium, separated from the scenes around the edge by the spirals of the sea. Round the edge are six scenes – at the sides Romulus, the Sabines, Mettus and Horatius; at the top the Capitol and at the bottom Catiline and Cato in the underworld. There are touches in this passage which lie outside pictorial art, but basically Virgil has presented it visually.

630–4.   **The mother wolf...:**   this first picture, of how the twins Romulus and Remus were suckled by a she-wolf, was perhaps the most famous of all Roman visual emblems, frequently depicted on coins.

635–41.   **The Sabine women...:**   the second picture shows the Rape of the Sabines. It is presented in two parts – first the violence, when the Romans carried off the Sabine women (whose king was Tatius) who were attending games at Rome; secondly the subsequent reconciliation leading to the appointment of the Sabine Numa as second king of Rome (cf. 6.808–11, with note).

642–5.   **Near this...:**   the third picture illustrates the horrifying penalty inflicted by the third king of Rome, Tullus Hostilius, on an Alban called Mettus who had promised aïd to the Romans, but defected to the enemy.

646–51.   **Porsenna...:**   the fourth picture depicts the attempt to restore the last Roman king, Tarquin the Proud, who had been expelled in 510 B.C. Lars Porsenna of Clusium, aided by some Romans, attacked the city but was thwarted by Horatius Cocles who held the bridge until it could be cut down, and then plunged into the Tiber. The story is told by Macaulay in his *Lays of Ancient Rome*:

Oh, Tiber! father Tiber!
To whom the Romans pray,
A Roman's life, a Roman's arms,
Take thou in charge this day! (*Horatius* LIX).

Cloelia was a hostage taken by Porsenna who escaped by swimming across the Tiber. The whole episode is designed to illustrate the unswerving bravery of the Romans of old.

652–66. Manlius ...: this scene at the top of the shield is in two sections: one shows the attack on the Capitol (defended by the Roman general Manlius) by the Gauls in 390 B.C. when the sacred geese gave the alarm; and the second shows religious ceremonies conducted by the priests (the Salii and Luperci) and by a procession of Roman matrons. What they have in common is the theme that the gods defend the god-fearing Romans: Livy (5.47) tells how at a time of famine the Romans had refrained from eating their sacred geese, and so they were saved by them at their hour of crisis.

652–3. Tarpeian fortress: see note on 347.

654. The palace, just built by Romulus ...: a better translation would be 'the palace built by Romulus being shown with a newly thatched roof'. This was a famous building on the Capitol hill whose thatch was constantly renovated.

664–5. The shields that fell from heaven: these were thought to have fallen from the sky during Numa's reign, and upon their safety depended Rome's survival. The Salii were the priests who guarded them.

666–70. Elsewhere the deep gates ...: this picture of the underworld is clearly at the bottom of the shield; it is in two parts, with Catiline in the area of the damned and Cato among the blessed. Catiline was a revolutionary whose conspiracy was defeated in 63 B.C.; Cato was a prominent statesman and Stoic philosopher of the same period, regarded (almost proverbially) as a pattern of justice.

676. The battle of Actium: this naval battle was the final battle of the civil wars in which Augustus defeated Antony and Cleopatra (31 B.C.) and was thus able to establish his sole rule over the Roman empire. It was off the western coast of Greece (cf. 3.274), just north of Cape Leucas.

679. The Italians: notice how Aeneas' enemies, the Italians,

91

have now become the supporters of Augustus. He is not 'leading the Trojans into battle'.

681.   **His father's star:**   a reference to the comet which appeared after Julius Caesar's death (he was the adoptive father of Augustus) which was believed to be carrying his soul to heaven. He was formally deified after his death.

682.   **Agrippa:**   a leading minister of Augustus; he was awarded a 'naval crown' for his earlier victories by sea in the civil wars.

686.   **Anthony:**   Marcus Antonius had allied with Octavian (the future Augustus) against the republicans Brutus and Cassius, but after they had been defeated the two became rivals for sole leadership of the Roman world. Anthony waged most of his campaigns in the East and formed an alliance with Cleopatra, queen of Egypt. Virgil presents the conflict very much from the Augustan point of view, yet perhaps allows a certain sympathy for Cleopatra (compare the superb ode which Horace wrote on the subject, 1.37).

697.   **Two serpents of death:**   a reference to the asps with which Cleopatra committed suicide when all was lost.

698.   **Anubis:**   a dog-headed god of the Egyptians; the ideological conflict is plainly portrayed here.

704.   **Apollo of Actium:**   Apollo was Augustus' special patron deity, and after his victory he restored Apollo's temple at Actium. Apollo is here portrayed in his capacity as the archer god.

707–13.   **You could see . . . :**   this is a second part of the picture, which is presented in three parts; the third has two separate scenes which begin at 714 and 720.

715.   **Three times a victor:**   Augustus ('Caesar', 714) celebrated a triple triumph in 29 B.C., for the battle of Actium, the Dalmatian war and the Alexandrian war.

716.   **Three hundred great shrines:**   one of the features of Augustus' reign was the building and restoration of temples to the gods.

720.   **Marble-white temple:**   the most famous of all Augustus' new temples, dedicated to Apollo in 28 B.C.; see note on 6.69f.

724–8.   **Nomads . . . Araxes:**   these conquered peoples range from Africa (Nomads, Africans), to Asia (Leleges, Carians, Euphrates, Araxes), Scythia (Gelonian, Scythians) and Gaul (Morini). The rivers are pictured as conquered too ('pacified', 'fretting about its bridge').

Book nine

In the ninth book the full-scale description of fighting begins, and continues until the end of the poem. The scenes of bloodshed are often based on Homer, and they have a more horrific effect because they are more tragic in Virgil. In Homer there is indeed pathos and sorrow for the dead, but war is accepted as a necessary and indeed almost natural part of the heroic world; in Virgil's time, especially to a peace-loving person like Virgil, it seemed inevitable perhaps but much less acceptable. Virgil has forced himself to portray the deeds of blood which had led to Aeneas' victory, and had indeed often been repeated by the Romans on their way to world empire, but he is unhappy with them. He is trying to convince himself and his readers that they are a necessary means to the end of world peace: he does not try to pretend that Rome grew great without them, but he portrays them in a way that emphasises the tragedy rather than the triumph.

The book begins with the strange supernatural description of how the Trojan ships were changed into sea-nymphs, and thereafter falls into two quite distinct battle stories. The first contains the grim deeds and deaths of Nisus and Euryalus, presented with an emotional pathos that is in many ways typical of Virgil; the second part describes the prowess of Turnus and the slaughter he dealt, and is far more objective and detached in its method. In the first the poet involves himself very personally in his narrative; in the second he stands back from it and in the Homeric mode allows the narrative to sweep along.

2 ff. **Juno sent down Iris . . .:**   Juno's intervention by means of Iris recalls 5.606 ff., where she causes the burning of the Trojan ships.

3. **The fiery Turnus:**   Turnus has been absent from the narrative since the opening of Book 8; he is reintroduced with a reference to his characteristic boldness and impetuosity.

10–11. **Etruscan . . . Lydian:**   after leaving Evander's city of Pallanteum, Aeneas went to Caere in the Etruscan territory to meet his allies. The Etruscans were thought to have come originally from Lydia in Asia Minor.

30–2. **Even as Ganges . . .:**   the point of the simile is the dispersed nature of the troops until they are marshalled into their due columns.

40–3. **Aeneas, that excellent soldier. . .:**   notice the emphasis on Aeneas' military forethought, contrasting strongly with Turnus' recklessness (cf. especially 757 ff.).

54–5. **Bloodcurdling war-cries:**   as Virgil comes to the full-scale description of warfare, he strongly emphasises the horror and terror of it (cf. the wolf simile in 59 ff.).

82. **Cybele:**   the mother of the gods (see 3.111–13) was worshipped especially on Mt. Berecynthus near Troy, where there were pine forests in abundance, suitable for making ships.

102–3. **Doto . . . Galatea:**   sea-nymphs; Nereus was a sea-deity.

104. **Stygian brother:**   Pluto. An oath by the river Styx was the most solemn that could be made (6.324).

119–20. **Plunged deep down like dolphins:**   this transformation of the Trojan ships into sea-nymphs (not found in the Aeneas legend before Virgil) is a strangely supernatural episode (cf. 110–113) set in the midst of the real world of siege and warfare. It seems to suggest that at the moment of fire and destruction there can still be escape and safety: it contrasts sharply with the realism and death of the rest of this book.

126. **But the fiery Turnus . . .:**   here we see the essence of the brave, impetuous, reckless leader of the Rutulians. The line is repeated at 10.276.

135–6. **The Fates and Venus . . .:**   Turnus' argument is that it was fated for the Trojans to arrive in Italy, and that fate is now fulfilled. There is no reason why they should survive their arrival.

138–9. **A resentment . . . can feel:**   Turnus compares himself with Menelaus and Agamemnon who sailed against Troy because of the rape of Helen. He too has lost his intended bride, Lavinia, and is equally prepared to fight for her.

140-2. **Let the Trojans say . . .:** Turnus imagines the Trojans as arguing that they have paid already for the rape of Helen; his answer is that they have now sinned in the same way again by trying to take Lavinia from him.

142-5. **It's quaint . . .:** Turnus is highly sarcastic about the feeble defences of the Trojan camp; even when they were defeated by the massive walls of Troy, built by Neptune, they could not hold out against the Greeks.

148. **Arms from Vulcan, or a thousand ships:** the Greeks sailed against Troy with a thousand ships, and their mightiest warrior, Achilles, had divine armour made for him by Hephaestus (Vulcan) when his own was lost after he had lent it to Patroclus.

149. **All the Etruscans:** see 10.

151. **Athene's image:** the sacred image of the goddess Pallas Athene, called the Palladium, upon whose preservation the safety of Troy depended (see note on 2.163). The line however is almost certainly spurious, in which case the translation of this sentence could be, 'The foe need fear no cowardly trickeries in the darkness, nor are we going to hide . . .'.

152. **A horse's dark paunch:** a reference to the strategem of the wooden horse, told at the beginning of Book 2.

154-5. **With Danaans or with Pelasgian troops:** i.e. Greeks, who took ten years to conquer Troy.

176-9. **Nisus . . . Euryalus:** these two friends had competed in the foot-race at the celebratory games for Anchises (5.294ff.): now they join together in a grimmer context. Their mutual love is reminiscent of that of Achilles and Patroclus in Homer. The episode that follows is a strange mixture of heroic devotion, violent murder and recklessness; it ends with very strong pathos as the death of the two friends is described, followed by the pitiful lamentations of Euryalus' mother.

184-5. **Is it God . . .?:** these famous lines summarise two ways of looking at the relationship between the human and the divine: for example, was it Venus who made Dido fall in love, or does Venus symbolise Dido's own inner love?

197-8. **The same great zest for glory:** this is exactly the motivation of the warriors in Homer.

218. **Acestes' city:** cf. 5.749ff., where Aeneas leaves behind the older folk in Sicily with his friend Acestes.

223. **The prince:** Aeneas' son Ascanius (233).

263ff. **I will give . . .:** the offering of gifts to reward bravery is again very much in the Homeric spirit: the quarrel of Achilles and Agamemnon (the main theme of the *Iliad*) revolves around the

95

recognition of a person's honour by prizes.

264. **The sack of Arisba:** nothing is known of this exploit of Aeneas'.

266. **Carthaginian Dido:** the mention of Dido introduces a note of foreboding; the only other place where she is mentioned in the second half of the poem is at the funeral of Pallas (11.74).

294. **At the image of filial love:** Euryalus' devotion to his mother is the kind of family tie which Ascanius feels for his father Anchises and his mother Creusa who died in Troy (2.771 ff.).

304. **Gnossos:** a town in Crete; the Cretans were famed for their craftsmanship.

314–449. **Sallying out ...:** this episode is exceptionally fast-moving; it is partly modelled on Homer. *Iliad* 10, but the scenes of violence in Virgil are even more horrifying, and the tragic ending typically Virgilian in its pathos.

367. **From the Latin city:** i.e. King Latinus' capital. We are not told its name; it may have been Laurentium.

387–8. **Called Alba, after Albanus:** better, 'called Alban, after Alba', i.e. the town of Alba gave its name to an area known as the Alban region.

405. **Latona's child:** Diana the huntress was also goddess of the moon, sometimes called Phoebe in this capacity (her brother Phoebus Apollo was god of the sun).

435–7. **So, when its stalk is cut ...:** the simile is based on a flower simile in Catullus; see the discussion of Virgil's sources in the Introduction.

446–9. **Ah, fortunate pair! ... :** an invocation of this kind to the characters in the poem is a very unusual feature, and indicates clearly what has been evident throughout, namely Virgil's emotional involvement in his story of the two heroic and reckless friends. The memory of Nisus and Euryalus has in the event outlasted by many centuries the house of Aeneas.

459. **Aurora ... Tithonus:** Tithonus was the mortal husband of Aurora, the dawn-goddess.

473 ff. **Meantime winged Rumour ...:** the description of the lamentation of Euryalus' mother recalls Andromache's grief for Hector in *Iliad* 22, and achieves an intense immediacy of pathos.

503 ff. **Then did the brazen tongue ...:** the remainder of the book is taken up with description of fierce fighting, especially centred on the prowess of Turnus. It is introduced with a reminiscence (503–4) of Ennius, Virgil's predecessor in Roman epic poetry, and it often recalls the battle scenes in Homer's *Iliad*, many of which centre round the deeds of valour (*aristeiai*) of particular prominent warriors.

96

The frequency of similes also recalls Homeric narrative.

525.   **Calliope:**   Muse of epic poetry.

563.   **The war-bird of Jove:**   i.e. the eagle.

590.   **Was the first time that Ascanius...:**   this is the only time in the poem when the young Ascanius takes part in the fighting (see also 656). It is particularly effective because of the arrogance of Numanus' taunts which lead Ascanius to vengeance.

598.   **Twice-captured Troy:**   see note on 2.643.

602.   **Atridae...Ulysses:**   Numanus taunts the Trojans rather as Turnus had done (137ff.), indicating that the Italians will be far more formidable than the Greeks.

603–13.   **We are brought up hard...:**   this picture of the early Italians corresponds to a large extent with the way the Romans liked to think of their ancestors.

614–20.   **But you ...:**   for the taunt against the Trojans of unmanliness cf. 4.215ff., 12.99. It is presented with vivid rhetorical force.

618–9.   **Dindymus...Cybele:**   the reference is to the emotional worship of Cybele on Mt. Dindymus or Mt. Berecynthus near Troy.

669.   **Goat-stars:**   the rising of these stars, in October, coincided with the time of autumn storms.

673.   **Dryad Iaera:**   a dryad is a wood-nymph; the sacred wood of Jupiter here referred to was on Mt. Ida near Troy.

691ff.   **Now Turnus ...:**   the mighty deeds of Turnus in the narrative which follows build up a picture of the formidable foe whom Aeneas will have to face on his return.

715–16.   **Prochyta...Inarime:**   islands near Baiae, a famous Roman spa near Naples. Typhoeus was a giant punished by being buried under the volcano on Inarime.

740.   **But Turnus, quite unflustered ...:**   the extreme self-confidence of Turnus on the battlefield is here seen very clearly.

742.   **Priam...Achilles:**   i.e. in the underworld he will meet the Trojan king Priam and tell him that Turnus' prowess was equal to that of Achilles who killed his son Hector. The equation of Turnus with Achilles had already been made by the Sibyl (6.89), and in many ways the arrogant Turnus is like a second Achilles fighting Aeneas as a second Hector, but this time destined to lose.

757–61.   **And if only the conquering Turnus...:**   here we see very clearly the defect in the impetuous Turnus; he is 'fighting-mad', and does not pause to think.

777.   **About war-horses...:**   the irony and pathos here are very strong: Cretheus was a singer who loved to sing of heroic deeds,

but was unable to perform them against Turnus.

789 ff. **Little by little . . .:** the picture of the slow retreat of Turnus against overwhelming odds is very closely reminiscent of that of Ajax in *Iliad* 16.102 ff.

816. **Into the river below:** we are reminded of Horatius Cocles who held the bridge until it was destroyed, and then leapt into the Tiber (8.650).

Book ten

Like the previous book, this is mainly concerned with fighting, and its centre deals with the confrontation of the young Pallas and the Rutulian general Turnus. The behaviour of Turnus in his one-sided victory is arrogant and offensive, even allowing for the heroic convention of boastfulness in triumph, and it paves the way for the dénouement of the poem, when Aeneas is about to spare Turnus' life, until he sees that Turnus is wearing the spoils which he took from Pallas (see Appendix 4). It is not the actual taking of spoils which is blameworthy: this was normal in the heroic way of life in Homer, and Pallas intended to do the same (445 ff.; though it should be noted that Aeneas dedicates to the gods spoils which he takes, rather than keeping them, 11.5 ff.). It is the manner of Turnus' triumph which alienates our sympathy.

Aeneas' reaction to the news of Pallas' death is violent in the extreme, and Virgil presents powerfully the mad anger which consumes his hero. The episode of the death of Lausus, near the end of the book, is in very marked contrast as Aeneas feels a wave of pity and a sense of the futility of bloodshed. This softer note is picked up at the beginning of Book 11, where the funeral of Pallas is described.

12. **Barbarous Carthage ... Alps:** this looks forward to the invasion of Italy by the Carthaginian Hannibal in 218 B.C.

16-95. **Venus in answer...:** the interchange of angry speeches between the rival goddesses is in marked contrast to the serenity of the opening scene of the council in heaven, and to Jupiter's calm reply (96 ff.). Both goddesses use all the tricks of rhetoric, especially irony and indignant questions; for a similar display of oratorical vehemence compare the speeches of Drances and Turnus in Book 11 (343 ff.).

28. **Diomed:** an embassy had been sent (8.9 ff.) to seek help from the famous Greek warrior (who came from Aetolia) now settled at Arpi in southern Italy.

33–5. **But if they were following...:** Venus' complaints are reminiscent of those she made earlier (1.234 ff.).

36–8. **Need I bring up again...?:** these are instances of Juno's intervention against the Trojans (5.606 ff., 1.50 ff., 9.2 ff.).

42. **Empire means nothing...:** this is of course highly sarcastic – Venus has directed her efforts throughout the poem to helping Aeneas to achieve the foundation of the Roman race.

51–2. **Amathus... Idalia:** the special places of Venus' worship. The irony continues throughout her speech, especially in the phrase 'unknown to fame', and the reference to Carthage crushing Italy, an unthinkable travesty of history.

61. **Xanthus and Simois:** rivers of Troy. Venus sarcastically suggests that Aeneas and his Trojans should return to Troy and be conquered again.

68. **Cassandra:** the prophetic daughter of Priam, cf. 2.246.

76. **Grandson of Pilumnus...:** Juno states Turnus' credentials; cf. 9.4 for Pilumnus, 6.90 for his goddess mother Venilia.

82. **A veil of cloud...:** a reference to how Venus saved Aeneas from Diomedes (Homer, *Iliad* 5.315 ff.).

83. **Transform his vessels...:** see 9.116 ff.

89. **Not the one:** i.e. the Trojan Paris ('Dardan philanderer', 92), who carried off Helen from Sparta.

109–10. **Whether the camp...:** Jupiter does not define why the Trojan camp is now besieged: it could be Italian destiny or a Trojan error.

113. **Fate will settle the issue:** here we see how Jupiter refuses to act one way or the other against fate. It is his responsibility to ensure that in the long term the decrees of fate are fulfilled; but fate may be delayed or even modified as a result of conflicting forces in heaven or the actions of mortals on earth. The relationship between fate and free-will in the *Aeneid* is essentially a paradoxical one, but the overall impression is that in spite of the predominance of destiny in the poem the actions of individual deities or humans are still of the utmost importance in determining how and when (and perhaps even whether) destiny will come true. As Camps says (p. 42): 'the texture, so to speak, of the ordinances of Fate is loose'. See also Otis, pp. 353–4.

The stream of his Stygian brother: an oath by Pluto's river, the

Styx, was the most sacred possible. This phrase and the next two lines are repeated from 9.104-6.

141. **Ismarus from Maeonia:** this area of Asia Minor included the river Pactolus, in which King Midas washed away his 'golden touch', thus making the river 'gold-bearing'.

143. **Mnestheus:** see 9.779ff.

145. **Capys:** linked etymologically with the famous and prosperous town of Capua in Campania.

155-6. **Heaven was with them ...:** it was necessary that they should have a foreign commander against the rebel Mezentius; see 8.503.

158. **Ida:** the figurehead of Mt. Ida, near Troy, reminds the Trojans of home.

163ff. **Now, Muses ...:** this catalogue of the allies of the Trojans is much shorter than the catalogue of Italian forces which concluded Book 7. The places named were all in Etruria, or (186ff.) further north.

189-93. **The legend being...:** Cycnus is the Latin word for the swan. The story was that he could not bear the loss of his beloved Phaethon (who was burnt when driving the Sun's chariot) and was metamorphosed into a swan (thus his fate, due to his love, was a 'reproach to Cupid and Venus'). Phaethon's sisters were turned into poplar trees (Ovid *Met.* 2.340ff.).

198-200. **Ocnus ... Mantua:** Mantua was Virgil's own home; Ocnus, its founder, sometimes called Bianor, was the son of the Tiber (Tuscan river) and Manto. Although well north of Etruria, it had strong connexions with the Etruscans.

206. **Mincius ... Benacus:** modern Mincio and Garda, the river on which Mantua stands and the lake into which it flows.

207. **Aulestes:** the brother of Ocnus (198).

220ff. **The nymphs, the ships ...:** see 9.77ff. Here, as there, Virgil briefly introduces the supernatural world of fanciful mythology in the midst of the reality of battle-scenes.

234. **The Mother:** the goddess Cybele, from whose pine-woods on Mt. Ida the fleet had been built (see 252).

238. **Arcadian cavalry:** a contingent sent by Evander by land, while Tarchon and Pallas and their troops sailed south by sea with Aeneas.

243. **Gold-rimmed shield:** the shield made by Vulcan for Aeneas, described at the end of Book 8.

253. **Dindymus:** a mountain near Troy. Cybele was associated with a turreted crown (6.784) and Phrygian lions (157).

260-2. **And now, as he stood ...:** the picture of Aeneas with his flashing armour standing high on his ship recalls the picture of Augustus on Aeneas' shield (8.678ff).

265. **Strymon:** a river in Thrace (cf. 11.580). Homer (*Iliad* 3.2ff.) has a simile of warriors moving to battle like a flight of cranes.

272. **A comet:** an oblique reference to Julius Caesar's comet (8.681). Compare Milton, *P.L.* 2.706–8: 'On th' other side, incensed with indignation Satan stood unterrified, and like a comet burned.'

273. **The fiery Dog-Star:** this part of the simile is based on one in Homer (*Iliad* 22.26ff.), where the armour of Achilles is compared with the brightness of the Dog-Star, portending disaster to his enemies.

276. **Yet the gallant Turnus ...:** the confidence of Turnus is expressed in the same phrase as in 9.126.

308–61. **Turnus reacted with speed...:** the battle description is rapid and Homeric in its method: it deals first with the Trojan successes and then (345ff.) with Italian successes.

310–11. **The yeoman ranks:** i.e. the supporters of Turnus are all country folk.

369–78. **Where are you running...:** Pallas' first speech to his men is like that of Ajax rallying the Greeks in Homer (*Iliad* 15. 733ff.).

378. **The sea, or Troy:** by Troy he means the Trojan camp which his troops are trying to relieve.

419. **The Fate-spinners laid their hands upon him:** i.e. on Halaesus, now that his father could no longer hide him.

438. **Their fates... greater foes:** the death of Pallas at Turnus' hands is described in the passage which follows; the death of Lausus at Aeneas' hands comes at the end of this book (808ff).

439. **His guardian sister:** the nymph Juturna, who plays a large part in Book 12.

442–3. **I am going alone... the duel:** this savage and arrogant remark by Turnus sets the tone of his behaviour in this episode (cf. 492, 500). The ancient commentator Servius describes it as *aspere et amare dictum* ('a harsh and bitter thing to say'). It is a crucial part of the poem because the spoils which Turnus strips from Pallas are the cause of his death in the final scene. Structurally it can be compared with the death of Patroclus at the hands of Hector in Homer (*Iliad* 16), which costs Hector his life when Achilles takes vengeance (*Iliad* 22). As will be seen, the final part of *Aeneid* 12 contains many reminiscences of *Iliad* 22. See also note on 501ff. and Otis p. 356.

447. **And truculent ...:** Pallas, just as much as Turnus, is portrayed in the confident boastful mood of the heroic warrior.

460-1. **Hercules...:** Evander had entertained Hercules (as is recounted in Book 8) when he was returning from Spain.

466. **To his son:** Hercules was the son of Jupiter and Alcmene.

468-9. **To enlarge his fame...:** compare Dryden, *Troilus and Cressida* 5.1: 'Our life is short but to extend that span to vast Eternity is virtue's work'.

470. **Sarpedon:** in Homer (*Iliad* 16.459 ff.) Zeus (Jupiter) wished to save his son Sarpedon, the Trojan warrior, but was forbidden by fate to do so.

496. **The sword-belt:** Turnus was wearing these spoils when he made his final appeal for mercy (12.942); because of them Aeneas refused him mercy.

497-8. **Engraved with a legendary crime...:** the reference is to the murder of the fifty sons of Aegyptus by the fifty daughters of Danaus at their father's instigation on the occasion of their wedding night (only Hypermnestra refused, cf. Horace, *Odes* 3.11); it is a story of horror and bloodshed appropriate for an emblem on the battlefield. Nothing is known of the artist Clonus.

501-9. **Ah, mind of man:** Virgil himself enters the narrative at this point, an unusual feature in epic poetry, first to make a general reflection on men's recklessness, and then (503 ff.) to anticipate the events at the end of the poem. The moral reflection expresses an idea very typical of Greek tragedy; Turnus in many ways is like the hero of a Greek tragedy, passing from happiness to disaster through a flaw in character (in Turnus' case arrogance). Virgil had similarly foreshadowed future events in the story of Dido (1.712, 4.169f.). Compare Milton's apostrophe to Adam and Eve (*P.L.* 4.366f.): 'Ah gentle pair, ye little think how nigh your change approaches ...'.

513 ff. **Mowing down all ...:** the description of Aeneas' reaction on the battlefield to the news of Pallas' death is savage in the extreme. His sense of grief and guilt causes him to lose control. Later his normal feelings of repugnance towards violence reassert themselves (821 ff.), but here he is as berserk and savage as any Homeric warrior, perhaps more so. See Camps pp. 28, 142 and Quinn pp. 223 ff.

516. **The banquet:** the reference is to Evander's friendly reception of Aeneas in Book 8.

517-8. **He captured alive four warrior sons:** this piece of barbarity is based on Achilles' actions in Homer (*Iliad* 21.27 ff., 23.175 ff.); it is even more horrifying in Virgil.

564. **Amyclae:** there was a story that because of frequent false alarms it was finally forbidden at Amyclae for anyone to sound an

alarm (of the enemy's approach) at all.

565.   **Aegaeon:**   his other name was Briareus (6.287), a giant of horrifying violence, such as Aeneas is now showing.

581–2.   **These aren't the horses of Diomed...:**   this is the taunt often thrown at the Trojans by the Italians, that they face a much more formidable foe than the Greeks who captured Troy.

606–88.   **Meanwhile, uninvited, Juppiter...:**   this episode acts as a break in the battle-scenes; it recalls the action of Apollo in Homer (*Iliad* 5.449 ff.), where he makes a phantom of Aeneas so that the real Aeneas may escape from Diomedes.

618.   **Pilumnus:**   Juno has made this point before (cf. 76).

661.   **But Aeneas:**   i.e. the real Aeneas is seeking Turnus, while Turnus has pursued the phantom Aeneas onto the ship.

688.   **The ancient town:**   i.e. Ardea, well to the south of the battlefield.

689 ff.   **Mezentius:**   the most savage of the Italians, see 7.647. This account of his *aristeia* is very Homeric, especially in the similes, and builds up his battle reputation so as to make him a formidable opponent for Aeneas.

705.   **Pregnant with fire:**   Hecuba before giving birth to Paris dreamed that she was pregnant by a blazing torch, cf. 7.319.

761.   **Tisiphone:**   one of the Furies, cf. 6.555.

763.   **Orion:**   the giant hunter, after whom a constellation was named.

775.   **A living trophy:**   spoils would normally be hung up in a temple as a trophy; in this case Lausus will receive the spoils and become a trophy himself. This contempt for the gods (the only god Mezentius worships is his own right hand, 773) was the quality stressed in Mezentius' first appearance in the poem (7.647).

791–3.   **How could I pass over...:**   again Virgil intervenes in his narrative (as he had for Pallas), to draw our special attention to the tragedy of youthful death (cf. 817 ff.).

817–18.   **Frail armour ... the tunic his mother had woven:**   thus Virgil emphasises the pathos of Lausus' death.

824.   **Filial devotion:**   Lausus shows towards his father Mezentius the same sort of devotion that Aeneas would show to Anchises. This feeling of pity in Aeneas (822) is very different from his mad anger immediately after Pallas' death (513 ff.).

827.   **These arms you were so proud of, keep them:**   this makes a specific contrast with the behaviour of Turnus when he had killed Pallas (495 ff.).

849–50.   **The bitterness of death:**   a better reading in my view would be 'the bitterness of exile', reading *exilium* rather than *exitium*.

Mezentius means that he has endured his exile cheerfully until this moment when he realises that it has 'tarnished' Lausus too.

852. **Since I was driven...:**   Mezentius refers to his exile from Etruria (8.489ff.; see note on 7.647).

856ff. **So saying, he struggles up ...:**   there is a certain splendour about the last-ditch courage of Mezentius, hateful character though he is. Quinn (p. 16) speaks of 'his icy, contemptuous acceptance of the calculated risks of war', and calls this passage 'a masterpiece of unsentimental pathos'.

880. **Nor yet will I spare your gods:**   i.e. Aeneas' prayer to Jupiter and Apollo (875) will be in vain; if they intervene Mezentius will confront them too.

900-6. **Harsh foe...:**   Mezentius' last words have an astringent realism, appropriate to the heroic code; see note on 856ff.

Book eleven

The book begins with a strong note of pathos, echoing the feeling of war's futility and horror which was dominant in the description of Lausus' death near the end of Book 10. The account of Pallas' funeral is presented in terms of muted sorrow; Aeneas' own genuine feelings of horror at war are seen here very clearly, and the mournful mood is reinforced by echoes of pathos from Catullus, by a reminiscence of Dido and by the tears of Pallas' war-horse. The sadness of the funeral itself is continued as the news of Pallas' death is taken to Evander and as the unnumbered dead are buried during the truce.

The mood of the next section (225-444) is entirely different. The rejection by Diomedes of the Latin embassy and Latinus' gloomy speech are succeeded by a rhetorical exchange between Drances and Turnus, a display of oratorical fireworks reminiscent of the vehement speeches of Venus and Juno at the beginning of Book 10. Here the reader's personal involvement is at its lowest point: as Drances and Turnus revile each other the interest is purely intellectual and detached.

Finally Virgil gives a long account of the battle-prowess and death of the warrior-maiden Camilla. This is in Homeric style (like the similar account of Turnus' deeds in the second half of Book 9), but the details of bloodshed and death are even more horrifying in Virgil than in Homer because they are less acceptable to him and he seems to be forcing himself to depict them. The brief scene describing Camilla's death abandons the objective style and is presented in the liquid notes of sorrow so typical of Virgil.

7. **He'd stripped from the enemy general:** notice how Aeneas consecrates the spoils of battle to Mars, unlike Turnus who had taken Pallas' armour for himself (10.500).

41. **Made by the spear of Turnus:** some editions of Day Lewis's translation erroneously have 'made by the spear of Mezentius'.

45 ff. **How different from all . . .:** notice how feelings of guilt and self-blame prey on Aeneas' mind (cf. 55 and note on 179).

58. **Lost to Ascanius:** because Pallas was like Ascanius a hope of the rising generation; Aeneas suggests that Pallas was almost a second son to him.

68–71. **And he resembles a flower. . .:** the simile recalls one in Catullus (11.22 ff.: 'destroyed like a flower at the meadow's edge, touched by the passing plough'; in moments of extreme pathos Virgil often recalls Catullus, cf. 9.435–7.

73. **Sidonian Dido:** again Virgil deepens the pathos by association, recalling the tragic events of *Aeneid* 4; line 75 is a repetition of 4.264. Cf. 97–8 and see note on 9.266.

81–2. **Manacled captives . . .:** see note on 10.517–8.

90. **It wept as it walked:** this is taken from Homer (*Iliad* 17.426 ff.), where Patroclus' horses weep at his death, and are comforted by Zeus: 'The horses were weeping when they heard that their charioteer had fallen in the dust at the hands of man-slaying Hector. . . the warm tears flowed from their eyes down to the ground, as they wept in longing for their charioteer'. Virgil has been extremely careful to build up the pathos to a high point before introducing this final touch.

96–7. **The same dread fate . . .:** Aeneas stresses the horror of the war which fate requires him to wage; see note on 111.

97–8. **Salute for evermore! For evermore, farewell:** these last words closely recall Catullus' poem at his brother's tomb (101.10: 'and for ever, my brother, hail and farewell'); see note on 73.

111. **Believe me, I'd like to make peace:** here we see very clearly Aeneas' hatred for war: it reminds us of the revulsion he felt after killing Lausus (10.821 ff.) and contrasts violently with his bloodlust when he heard of the death of Pallas (10.513 ff.).

113. **It is not your people . . .:** compare the similar sentiments which Aeneas expresses in 12.190f.

122. **Drances:** this spokesman of the peace party is portrayed as a shifty and unpleasant character, thus increasing our sympathy for Turnus. As Quinn says, Drances is on the right side for the wrong reasons.

179. **Vengeance on Turnus:** this last request of Evander,

putting a powerful obligation on Aeneas, has to be remembered when in the final scene of the poem Aeneas does take vengeance. Virgil invites us to consider whether Aeneas was justified in fulfilling this obligation.

208.   **They burnt them, uncounted, anonymous**:   this phrase crystallises the sense of futility and sorrow which has been so powerfully built up in the whole of this passage by means of the long description of funeral rites. Sorrow over the dead in Homer is not presented with quite this kind of intensity.

225 ff.   **In the middle of these cross-currents . . .**:   the next 200 lines are taken up with four speeches: the factual report of the envoys, the proposals of the gloomy Latinus, and then the violent rhetoric of Drances' attack on Turnus and Turnus' reply.

227.   **From Diomed's city**:   these envoys had been sent (8.9ff.) to ask for aid from the Greek warrior now settled in Italy, who might be expected to give aid against his old enemies the Trojans.

239.   **Aetolian**:   Diomedes originally came from Aetolia before moving to Argos (244) and then to Italy (Arpi, 246).

245.   **The hand ... Ilium**:   an exaggerated account of Diomedes' contribution to the destruction of Troy.

247.   **Apulian Garganus**:   an area of southern Italy.

258 ff.   **Suffered condign and terrible retribution . . .**:   Diomedes now gives a list of the disasters which befell the Greek warriors on their return from Troy: Ajax son of Oileus was shipwrecked by Athene (see note on 1.39); Menelaus was driven to Egypt, where Proteus was king (this is the subject of Euripides' *Helen*); Ulysses (Odysseus) wandered for ten years in his efforts to return home and was nearly eaten by the Cyclops (see note on 3.613); Neoptolemus, son of Achilles, died after a brief rule in Epirus (3.333f.); Idomeneus was driven out of Crete (3.121f.); the Locrians were followers of Ajax son of Oileus, evidently driven to Africa after Ajax's death; Agamemnon was murdered by his wife Clytemnestra and her lover Aegistheus, as is told in Aeschylus' *Oresteia* trilogy.

270.   **Calydon**:   a town in Aetolia where Diomedes originally lived.

272.   **Changed into birds**:   this metamorphosis (cf. Ovid, *Met.* 14.497 ff.) was due to an insult offered to Venus, who consequently changed some of Diomedes' comrades into swans.

277.   **Wounding the hand of Venus**:   this refers to the encounter of Diomedes with Aphrodite (Venus) in Homer (*Iliad* 5.334ff.).

283.   **Have met him hand to hand**:   the contest between Diomedes and Aeneas was described in Homer (*Iliad* 5.239ff.).

Diomedes builds up a picture of Aeneas' military prowess which surpasses the Homeric account.

292. **Stood first in devotion of heart:** this is Aeneas' special quality (*pietas*), which had impressed even the enemy. The picture of Aeneas which Diomedes gives here accords much more with Virgil's Aeneas than with Homer's.

302ff. **I could wish ...:** the speech of Latinus, urging peace with the Trojans, puts added blame on Turnus for wishing to continue the war, however much we may sympathise with Turnus' courage.

307. **Though beaten, they never ...:** exactly the same sentiments about the Romans are put by Livy (27.14.1) into the mouth of Rome's greatest enemy, Hannibal.

318. **The Sicilians' frontier:** this is a people called the Sicani, settled in Central Italy.

336ff. **Then Drances ...:** the speech of Drances is a piece of high-flown rhetoric; it arouses in the reader a sense of horrified expectation about how Turnus will reply, and serves to vary the mood of pathos and sorrow which the battle-scenes in this part of the poem inspire.

376. **Intransigent:** this word represents the Latin word *violentia*, a word used in the *Aeneid* several times of Turnus, but of no one else.

396. **Bitias and huge Pandarus:** Turnus refers to his successful break-in to the Trojan camp (9.672ff.).

403. **The Myrmidon generals ...:** as an example of something equally impossible to imagine Turnus suggests that the greatest Greek warriors, with their troops of Myrmidons, were terrified of the Trojans; or else that rivers should flow backwards.

410. **Now, sire ...:** Turnus has now finished with Drances, and turns to address King Latinus.

429-33. **Messapus ... Tolumnius ... Camilla ...:** this enumeration of the brave warriors on the Italian side is splendidly impressive. Messapus occurs fairly frequently as a leading Italian warrior; Tolumnius the augur appears again at 12.258ff. The exploits of the warrior-maiden Camilla (432; see note on 7.803ff) occupy most of the rest of this book.

439. **Made by Vulcan himself:** see note on 8.626ff.

471-2. **He censured himself ...:** the worried guilt-laden feelings of Latinus contrast very strongly with the wild impetuosity of Turnus. Latinus had in fact accepted Aeneas and offered him the hand of Lavinia (7.259ff.) but his intentions were thwarted by the outbreak of war.

492-7.   **So, when a horse...:**   this simile is very appropriate for expressing the excitement of Turnus as he prepares for war (cf. 12.81ff.). It is based closely on a simile used twice by Homer (*Iliad* 6.506ff. and 15.263ff.), and imitated by Ennius.

532ff.   **Meanwhile, in the abodes ...:**   the action involving Turnus and his ambush is now held in suspense as Virgil turns to narrate the prowess of Camilla. Before doing so he sets the background to her battles by painting a scene in heaven between the maiden goddess Diana (Camilla's patron goddess) and her nymph Opis. It provides a pastoral prelude to the fierce war-scenes which follow.

611.   **Darkening the very sky:**   compare the story in Herodotus (7.226) of how the Spartans were told that the spears of their Persian enemy would be so numerous that they would blot out the sun. They replied: 'Then we shall be able to fight in the shade'.

648ff.   **Right in the thick...:**   this account of the battle-prowess of Camilla is very much in the Homeric tradition (and in many ways reminiscent of Turnus' prowess in Book 9): there are numerous such *aristeiai* in the *Iliad* (Achilles, Hector, Diomedes, Patroclus, Idomeneus etc.). Virgil has presented it (except for the very last scene) in the manner of Homer, i.e. a fast-moving narrative where the facts speak for themselves, rather than in his other manner of subjective involvement in the suffering and pathos (as for example with Nisus and Euryalus, or Lausus). Camilla is Virgil's own creation, partly based on Amazon warriors like Penthesilea (1.490). She is a strange mixture of the beauty of an idyllic pastoral world (cf. the description of her in 7.803ff.) and the heroic world of violence and cruelty (cf. the simile of the falcon and the dove, 721-4, taken from Homer, *Iliad* 22.139ff., where it is used of Achilles).

701.   **Ligurian tricksters:**   the Ligurians, who lived in the territory around the northern Apennines, had a reputation for trickery.

727.   **The Etruscan, Tarchon:**   he was leader of the whole Etruscan contingent that came to aid the Trojans (8.603f.).

759ff.   **Now Arruns ...:**   the portrayal of the stealthy and sinister Arruns is unfavourable in the highest degree.

779.   **Or to strip off his gold...:**   the final downfall of Camilla is due to her desire for fine booty (compare Euryalus in Book 9, whose death was caused by the flashing light from a helmet which he had taken as spoils); observe how long a description Virgil has given to Chloreus' splendid attire.

785.   **Apollo ... Soracte:**   Mt Soracte in Etruria was a famous seat of Apollo's worship, which was particularly strong in Etruria.

823 ff.   **Acca, dear...:**   after the gusto and violence of Camilla's battle-deeds her death is portrayed softly and gently. The line describing her death (831) is the same as the last line of the *Aeneid*, describing Turnus' death.

913.   **The roseate sun:**   the book ends with the Italians in desperate straits, but the army of Turnus still intact. Thus the stage is set for the final confrontations in the last book.

Book twelve

In the final book the preparations for a single combat are made, but the truce is broken and full-scale fighting breaks out. The Trojans are successful and finally Turnus accepts once more that he must fight Aeneas. He is wounded, and when he begs for mercy, Aeneas – taking vengeance for Pallas' death – refuses it.

Throughout this book Virgil has used the Homeric story of the duel between Achilles and Hector as a background to his own story. Turnus has frequently been equated with Achilles in the poem; but this time the Achilles figure is in the losing situation against the Trojan. The similarities are very marked: the death of Pallas at Turnus' hands is closely parallel with the death of Patroclus at Hector's hands (*Iliad* 16), and the final stages of the single combat seem in many ways like a replay of Homer's story, this time with the roles reversed. Because all through the poem we have seen Aeneas as a Homeric warrior trying to learn a different set of values of a proto-Roman kind, we feel confident that when Turnus begs for mercy we shall see the difference from Achilles' savage rejection of Hector's pleas; but in fact Aeneas behaves exactly as Achilles does, and his helpless opponent is killed. The poem ends on a note of confusion and uncertainty.

Various reasons may be put forward in justification of Aeneas' action, but Virgil has given only one: the desire for revenge. When Turnus so savagely killed Pallas (10.441 ff.) Virgil prophesied that a time would come when he would bitterly regret it; but when the time does come it is impossible to feel happy about it. Virgil knew that vengeance was a part of Roman history (Augustus had taken vengeance for Julius Caesar on all his assassins), but whether it was justifiable was another question. Virgil has forced himself and us to face this dilemma (it would have been so easy to end the poem with a mortal wound inflicted on Turnus, eliminating the question of mercy), and he has presented it in such a way as to concentrate our attention at the very end of the poem not on Aeneas' triumph but on the death of Turnus: 'With a deep sigh   The unconsenting spirit fled to the shades below'. For a fuller discussion of the final scenes see Appendix 4.

9.   **So Turnus looks:**   at the beginning of the final book Virgil emphasises the qualities which we already associate with Turnus – bravery, anger and impetuous violence.

18 ff.   **Latinus would not be rushed . . .:**   the efforts of Latinus and Amata to dissuade Turnus from facing Aeneas are reminiscent of those of Priam and Hecuba in *Iliad* 22 as they try to dissuade Hector from facing Achilles. This is the first of many reminiscences of Homer in this book, so that we see Turnus (the new Achilles figure) in the situation of Homer's Hector: this time the successor of the Greek conqueror is to be defeated by the Trojan.

45.   **Ardea:**   the home (in southern Italy) of Turnus' father, Daunus.

52.   **His goddess mother . . .:**   a reference to how Aeneas was saved by his mother in Homer (*Iliad* 5.311 ff.). Compare 10.82.

64.   **Lavinia:**   the princess is a very shadowy figure, who rarely appears and never speaks; she is the *casus belli* rather than a character in her own right.

84.   **Orithyia . . . Pilumnus:**   Orithyia was the wife of the North Wind; Pilumnus (9.4) was an ancestor of Turnus.

87 ff.   **Turnus then put . . .:**   the twenty-line description of Turnus getting his armour ready, concluding with the simile of the bull, conveys again the essential nature of Turnus. He is a mighty warrior, at his best in war, and happy at the prospect. By contrast the description of Aeneas getting ready (107 ff.) is brief and matter-of-fact: Aeneas is grimly determined to do what must be done.

138.   **Juturna:**   Turnus' sister had been made a nymph-goddess by Jupiter after he had made love to her. There was a lake called Juturna near the Alban hill, and a temple to her in Rome in Virgil's time.

158.   **Or start them all fighting:**   by this brief episode between Juno and Juturna Virgil instils a sense of foreboding during the description of the oaths which follow.

164. **His ancestor the Sun:** according to one version of the legend Latinus was descended from Circe, daughter of the Sun.

175. **Aeneas the true:** the single combat with Turnus is the final act required of Aeneas as man of destiny (the Latin word is his standing epithet, *pius*).

189-94. **I shall not make ...:** notice that Aeneas' terms are very moderate.

198. **Janus:** the two-headed god Janus was especially associated with treaties (cf. 7.610).

219-21. **Turnus heightened the feeling ...:** Virgil here broadens the character of Turnus by indicating that at this final solemn moment his impetuous recklessness has been diminished.

281. **Caeretans:** Etruscans from Caere.

296. **He's had it:** an expression used at the death-blow of gladiators.

311-17. **But Aeneas the true ...:** here Aeneas makes his last endeavour for peace. Without weapons or helmet he rushes onto the battlefield, urging an end to violence (313). But his essential hatred of violence is overborne by passionate anger after his wound has been healed (441 ff.) as it is again in the final scene of the poem.

331-6. **As, by the banks ...:** the simile of the war-god Mars is set in Thrace (northern Greece), traditionally associated with war. It is based on two passages in Homer (*Iliad* 13.298 ff.), where the warrior Idomeneus is compared with the war-god, and *Iliad* 4.440 ff., where the retinue of Mars is described – 'Terror and Fear and Strife ...'). Thus this account of Turnus' prowess, like the previous one in the second half of Book 9, invites us to see him as in every way a Homeric warrior, unlike Aeneas who is sometimes Homeric, sometimes not.

347. **The war-famed son of that Dolon ...:** the story is told in Homer (*Iliad* 10) of how Dolon, son of Eumedes and father of this Eumedes, attempted to spy out the Greek camp, but was killed by Odysseus and Diomedes.

365-70. **As when a northerly gale ...:** again the simile is from Homer (*Iliad* 11.305 ff.); see note on 331 ff.

394. **Of divination ...:** these are three of Apollo's special skills; medicine too (396) was one of his attributes (he was the father of Asclepius, god of medicine).

419. **Ambrosia ... panacea:** juices associated with the immortals.

436. **From others, the meaning of fortune:** a clearer translation would be 'good luck from others'. Throughout the poem Aeneas has been battered by the blows of hostile fortune, and like a

good Stoic endeavoured to stand up to them. He hopes that Ascanius will have better fortune.

451–5. **As when a storm has burst . . .:** this is the traditional translation, but I think it more likely that the meaning is 'as when the sun's light is cut off'. This simile too (see note on 331ff.) is based on Homer (*Iliad* 4.275ff.), indicating that Aeneas' behaviour, under the stimulus of his wound, is on this occasion to be of the pattern of the Homeric warrior – we shall see no mercy or pity from him on this occasion (cf. 494ff., where the deeds of Aeneas and Turnus are related side by side, with little difference between them).

517–20. **Menoetes . . .:** this little cameo is typically Virgilian; the humble fisherman from Arcadia, with no pretensions to be a warrior, is killed like the rest.

521–5. **You know how it is . . .:** again both similes are from Homer (*Iliad* 11.155ff., 4.452ff.).

542 ff. **Aeolus:** again (cf. 517ff.) Virgil focusses attention on the pathos of death.

582. **Twice the Italians . . .:** once on the occasion of the outbreak of the war (7.591ff.), once after the truce in this book.

645–9. **What? Turn my back? . . . :** here we see Turnus at his finest, facing the hour of death with the bravery required from him by his knowledge of his personal responsibility to do nothing unworthy (cf. 668).

666–8. **Speechless and staring . . .:** the news of the attack on the Latin capital and the queen's suicide leave Turnus dazed, like the hero in a Greek tragedy battered by the blows of fortune for which his own actions have been partly responsible. As with Dido, so with Turnus: the pressure of events bows a head which it had seemed could never be bowed.

684–9. **Even as a boulder . . .:** once more the simile is based on one in Homer (*Iliad* 13.137ff., describing Hector).

701–3. **Gigantic as Athos . . .:** the comparison is with the size of mountains (first Mt. Athos in Greece, then Mt. Eryx in Sicily, and finally the Italian Appennine range), but there are additional points of comparison in the noise of the storm, and the joy of the Appennines.

715. **As on the ranges of Sila . . .:** notice how, as so often, Virgil gives a geographical location to his simile, thus adding an extra touch of realism. Sila and Taburnus were Italian mountains.

725–7. **Juppiter holds the scales . . .:** after the frequent reminiscence of Homeric similes in this book Virgil now begins a series of echoes from the decisive single combat in the *Iliad* between Achilles and Hector. This image is based on *Iliad* 22.209ff., where

Zeus balances the fates of the two contestants and Hector's is the losing one.

749-57. Like the scene when a hound . . .: this simile is based on *Iliad* 22.185ff.

763-5. Five times the pair ran . . .: this is a very close reminiscence of *Iliad* 22.158ff.: 'In front a good man fled, but a much better one pursued him swiftly; for they were not contending for a beast of sacrifice or a bull's hide, such as are men's prizes for running, but they ran for the life of Hector, tamer of horses'.

790. Stand facing each other: thus Virgil halts the mortal action prior to his description of the resolution of the conflict on the divine plane in the passage which follows.

795. As a national hero: the Latin word (*indiges*) suggests one who because of his service to his people is deified, and becomes a divine emblem of their destiny.

823-8. Do not command . . .: the requests which Juno makes are highly important ones; that the people to be formed by union of Trojans and Latins should (i) be called Latins, not Trojans; (ii) speak Latin and not Trojan; (iii) keep the Latin way of dress. Jupiter grants these requests (833-8) and enlarges them by changing 'dress' into 'old traditions'. Thus Juno, the implacable enemy throughout the poem, is paradoxically responsible for the greatness of the Romans, who were in the end most certainly Latins rather than Trojans.

827. The qualities making it great be Italian: so indeed they were.

830-1. Jove's sister . . .: this domestic touch is reminiscent of Zeus and Hera in Homer. Jupiter as son of Saturn himself recognises the power of the emotion which his sister feels.

835-6. The Trojans will but sink down . . .: i.e. in the union of the two races the Trojans will be the recessive element.

836-7. I'll add the rites . . .: i.e. the religious ceremonies of the Italians will not be superseded by those of the Trojans but harmonised with them. Aeneas has brought his gods with him from Troy, but they will be made to fit in with the existing Italian religion. In Virgil's day the time-honoured traditions of religious ceremony were thought of as having Italian origins far more than Trojan origins.

839. Nay even the gods, in godliness: this extravagant and paradoxical phrase indicates the great emphasis which the Romans throughout their history placed on their religion. They were clear that their supremacy in the world was due to divine favour caused by their subservience to their gods: in Horace's phrase (*Odes* 3.6.5), addressing the Romans, 'Because you are servants of the gods you are rulers on earth'.

840.   **No other nation . . .:**   thus Juno the enemy of the Trojans becomes Juno the great patron goddess of the Romans, queen of heaven in the Roman hierarchy. Her temple on the Aventine was restored by the Emperor Augustus.

843 ff.   **This being accomplished . . .:**   after the agreement in heaven, there still remains the question of detaching Juturna's divine aid from Turnus; rather than instructing Juno to do so Jupiter acts in the most decisive way by sending a Fury from Hell to achieve his purpose.

845.   **Two demon fiends:**   the three Furies were Megaera (847), Allecto and Tisiphone. Virgil does not state which of the two latter was chosen by Jupiter.

862.   **The shape of that small owl:**   there is a terrifying and demonic tone about this passage; it recalls the apparition of the owl at Dido's visit to her dead husband's shrine (4.457 ff.).

872 ff.   **Oh, Turnus . . .:**   Juturna's speech of lamentation is reminiscent in several ways of Anna's lament over Dido's death: 871 is exactly the same as 4.673.

891.   **Proteus:**   a sea-deity able to change himself into all kinds of shapes (*Georgics* 4.440 ff.).

908–12.   **As it is in a nightmare . . .:**   this is the last of the many reminiscences of Homer's description of the combat between Achilles and Hector; cf. *Iliad* 22.199 ff.: 'As in a dream a man cannot pursue the man who runs away – the one cannot catch him, nor the other get away – so Achilles could not catch Hector, nor Hector get away'.

931.   **I've deserved it:**   Turnus does not mean that he accepts any moral guilt, but that in a single combat the loser must accept his defeat.

939.   **He did not strike:**   the reader's strong expectation at this point is that Aeneas will show himself different from Achilles in Homer, who had savagely and mercilessly killed the suppliant Hector. It comes therefore as a savage shock when Aeneas behaves exactly like Achilles.

942.   **The fatal baldric:**   cf. 10.495 ff., where Turnus strips the sword-belt from the dead Pallas.

949.   **In retribution:**   Virgil makes it very clear that vengeance is the cause of Aeneas' action. Whether it is justifiable in all the circumstances he does not make clear.

952.   **The unconsenting spirit:**   the poem ends, not with the triumph of Aeneas who has at long last after many trials and disasters achieved his divine mission of founding Rome, but with the death of Turnus, the victim (like Dido) of Rome's mission.

Themes
Augustus lineage - Julian
Destiny of Rome to rule the world by
  a) military conquest
  b) peace
) Keeping of the faith
) Maintainance of family
    values
) Gates of war to be closed

① Destiny in Homer and Virgil
② Aeneas to establish
    a) a city
    b) a way of life
③ Roman ideals
    a) law
    b) religion
    c) settled life

Appendix

1. Analysis of 1.257–96

Jupiter's speech

The speech of Jupiter in reply to his daughter's complaints is one of the great patriotic passages in the poem (others are 6.756ff. and 8.626ff.). It is all the more emphatic because it is set in a framework of episodes based on Homer's *Odyssey*, and yet is itself totally unhomeric, thus underlining the main difference between Virgil's poem and its Homeric models – namely the theme of destiny working through long ages for the benefit of humankind. Destiny indeed is a frequent concept in Homer, but always short-term, affecting the lives of individuals; but in Virgil Jupiter, as the agent of destiny, has a plan reaching forward through many generations for the ultimate happiness and prosperity of the world, provided that his chosen agents, Aeneas and all the Romans to come, are prepared and strong enough to play their parts.

The speech begins with reassurance for Venus and the promise of immortality for Aeneas. It then details the events described in the second half of the poem, in which Aeneas defeats the Rutulians and establishes 'city walls and a way of life'. This phrase summarises the nature of the Roman mission of which Aeneas is the chosen instrument: first he is to found his city with its defensive walls to ensure physically the survival of the Trojan–Italian people who will be the ancestors of the Romans; and secondly and most important he has to establish 'a way of life'. That is to say that the old Trojan way of life will not do; a proto-Roman set of values has to be established. The Latin word used is *mores*, which has the moral implication of civilisation, and entails the Roman ideals of law and religion and settled life, to be developed by the Romans themselves and then, after military conquest, to be bestowed on the world.

Jupiter continues to describe the future; Aeneas will rule for only three years (the legend of his death is very vague and mysterious) and then the dynasty will pass to his son, Ascanius. His other name Iulus

119

is here linked with his Trojan origins (Ilium), as it is to be linked with his descendants of the famous Julian family (287), into which Augustus, the first Roman emperor, was adopted. He will move the kingdom from the first settlement Lavinium to Alba Longa, where kings of the same dynasty will rule for 300 years before the time comes for the foundation of Rome itself. By this chronological device Virgil bridges, or nearly bridges, the gap between the traditional date of the fall of Troy (1184 B.C.) and the foundation of Rome (753 B.C.).

Jupiter now comes to the foundation of Rome itself by Romulus, the son of Mars and Ilia, who survived exposure by being suckled by a she-wolf (cf. 8.630 ff). At this point he expresses in sonorous phrases the imperial destiny of Rome: 'No bounds, either in space or time; unlimited power...'. These phrases would have excited the patriotic pride of Virgil's readers, and perhaps inspired them to feel that they must show themselves worthy of so majestic a divine mission. The great enemy Juno, whose opposition to the Trojans causes most of the bloodshed and suffering in the poem, will be reconciled; as indeed she is (12.791 ff, especially 840), and she becomes a leading deity in Roman religious worship.

When Jupiter refers to the Romans (282) as 'the lords of creation, the togaed people', he again makes the double point that was made in 'city walls and a way of life' (264). The first aspect of the mission is military conquest and imperial rule ('lords of creation'); the second is to give the benefits of peace and settled civilisation to the conquered ('the togaed people' means that the Romans will have discarded their military uniform, and put on instead the toga, garment of civilian life).

From the whole of Roman history Jupiter now selects only two periods: the first (283 ff.) refers specially to Aeneas and promises vengeance on the Greeks who have just burned Troy to ashes, killing many of his friends. The terms used to depict Rome's conquest of Greece (which took place in the second century B.C.) are those appropriate to the heroic age in which Aeneas lived (Agamemnon, Diomed, Achilles, Argos).

The second period is Virgil's own time, the reign of the emperor Augustus. The Caesar referred to is certainly Augustus (not Julius Caesar, as some commentators have maintained), and it is prophesied that his empire will reach to the ends of the earth (particularly in

120

the East, where Augustus fought his final battles) and that he himself will be deified after death. The vision of the idyllic world which he will rule over (291-6) is one of the most optimistic statements of Rome's new Golden Age to be found anywhere. Virgil and his contemporaries had certainly lived through an 'age of violence' (291) during the long civil wars, and had high hopes that under Augustus it was indeed 'mellowing into peace'. The personification of 'venerable Faith' has a special reference to Roman ideals in which the breaking of faith was one of the worst sins, and the epithet 'venerable' suggests the long traditions of Rome to which the people of the Augustan Age aimed to return. The 'Home' represents the very centre of Roman moral values, with their enormous emphasis on the importance of the family (reflected in the *Aeneid* by Aeneas' relationship with his father Anchises and his son Ascanius). The reference to Romulus and Remus is another reference to peace and reconciliation: the twins had quarrelled when Remus jumped over the wall which Romulus built round his new city, and Romulus in anger slew him. This was used as a symbol of Rome's civil wars (cf. Horace, *Epodes* 7, a poem expressing guilt over civil strife and ending: 'Bitter destiny pursues the Romans and the crime of the slaughter of brothers ever since the blood of innocent Remus, a curse to posterity, was spilled on the ground'). Here then Romulus and Remus will be re-united. The 'grim, steel-welded gates of War' were in the Temple of Janus, and had been open (indicating a state of war) throughout almost all Rome's tempestuous history. But under Augustus, for the first time for two hundred years, they were closed: Jupiter here promises that they will remain closed. Finally Jupiter presents a vivid visual personification of the 'spirit of Discord' chained and helpless, unable to use the armaments in which it had delighted. The Latin word here translated as 'Discord' is *Furor*, the irrational element in man's character which leads to uncontrolled and frenzied behaviour. Throughout the *Aeneid* Aeneas battles to overcome this quality, both in himself and in others, with only very imperfect success; Jupiter promises that one day the Romans will succeed in overcoming it.

2. Analysis of 4.584-629

The passage begins with a serene and beautiful description of dawn, presented in the rich mythology of the goddess Aurora and her husband Tithonus. These two opening lines present a striking contrast to the agonising wretchedness of Dido, alone and isolated in

121

her watch-tower, observing the final frustration of all her hopes and desires, defiling her beauty in her uncontrolled misery.

She begins with angry and sarcastic phrases, bitterly resentful that she has been mocked, slighted; she is consumed by injury to her pride and calls on her people to avenge her by military action. But she is alone, nobody hears her, she has no audience. She suddenly realises this ('What am I saying? . . .') and utters words of self-reproach, before returning to sarcastic reviling of Aeneas. Then, as fury consumes her, she thinks of the vengeance which she might have taken, but now cannot; she uses the most horrifying and grotesque of Greek myths to express her unrestrained hatred. Littering the sea with Aeneas' limbs recalls the story of Medea tearing her young brother Apsyrtus apart and scattering the pieces on the waves to delay the pursuit of the Colchians; serving up Ascanius to his father at a banquet is a reminiscence of how Atreus served up his children to Thyestes. It is beyond belief that the admirable and sympathetic queen whom we met in Book 1 should utter these blood-curdling sentiments.

Dido dwells on what she might have done in the past ('I should have stormed . . .'). She no longer has power to do any of these things; she can only regret that when she could have done them, she failed to do so.

At this point in her soliloquy Dido pauses and gathers herself for a slow and solemn invocation ('O sun, with your beams. . .') to all the powers which could help her: first the all-seeing sun, then her patron goddess Juno, goddess of Carthage and goddess of marriage; then Hecate, the witch of the underworld; then the Avenging Furies, who can give her that vengeance on Aeneas which her broken pride craves; and finally all possible divinities that will aid ('the patrons of dying Elissa'). And she goes on to demand revenge, in a series of curses upon Aeneas all of which in some measure came true. He was indeed 'harried in war' by Turnus and the Italians; he had to leave Ascanius while he went to Evander to sue for aid; he saw his friends dying; he accepted the terms of a harsh peace when Juno secured an agreement that the Italians should be the dominant partners in the Trojan–Italian agreement; and he lived only a few years after he founded his city; his death was mysterious and his body was never found.

But Dido has not yet finished: from her particular curses upon Aeneas she turns to a wider prospect and asks that her Carthaginians shall inherit from her a heritage of undying hostility towards the Romans. This, not a tribute of flowers or a religious offering, is the present she wishes for upon her death. She calls on an unnamed avenger: the Romans would obviously identify him as Hannibal, the Carthaginian who came nearest of all Rome's enemies to destroying her. For several generations the Romans and the Carthaginians fought fiercely and bitterly for the leadership of the Mediterranean world. Dido's personal anger is generalised into the long pages of history: her hatred lived on long beyond her death and her call for vengeance was amply fulfilled by the destruction of those countless Romans who fell in the wars against Carthage.

3. Analysis of 6.445-76

Aeneas' encounter with the ghost of Dido is one of the most moving passages in the *Aeneid*, and Virgil has used all his skill in its construction, especially by enriching it with literary echoes. It begins with one of Virgil's favourite devices: a crowd scene (445-9), followed by a spot-light on a single character (compare the treatment of the Deiphobus episode, first a crowd-scene, 479-493, then a spot-light on Deiphobus; the device is also used in the pageant of heroes, 6.760ff.). Our interest is not greatly aroused by the summary list of seven heroines (Phaedra etc.) none of whom (except Pasiphae, briefly) figures otherwise in the *Aeneid*; consequently the mention of the eighth, Phoenician Dido, who has so dominated the poem up to now, has a tremendous impact. The reader may not be much moved by the fate of Phaedra or Procris, but he has shared Dido's suffering all through Book 4.

The encounter begins with a simile of the moon's dim light, adapted from Apollonius Rhodius (4.1479-80), a poet whom Virgil had often recalled in *Aeneid* 4. Apollonius' account of the love-story of Jason and Medea had been the first intimate analysis in epic poetry of the emotions of love, and had set a precedent for Virgil's subjective involvement with Dido. Thus the simile helps to take us back again into that world of intimate emotion.

Aeneas' speech begins with the epithets 'poor, unhappy' (*infelix*, an epithet often applied by Virgil to Dido in Book 4, and finally used by Dido of herself as Aeneas leaves her (4.596)). It continues with other reminiscences of Book 4 as Aeneas once again, for the last time, tries to explain to Dido why he had to leave her – compare 460 with 4.361, 461-3 with 4.356-8, 466 with Dido's words in 4.314 (Dido had said, 'Are you running away from me?', and Aeneas says, 'Don't run away from me').

In Dido's flint-like immovability we are reminded of the accusation she had made against Aeneas' flint-like hardness (4.367); and in her refusal to speak Virgil powerfully and irresistably recalls a famous scene in Homer (*Odyssey* 11.563 ff.) where Odysseus speaks to the ghost of Ajax (who had committed suicide because Odysseus had beaten him in the contest for the armour of Achilles); Odysseus says he is sorry that he had been the cause of Ajax's death, and Ajax turns away without replying.

Thus we see how in this brief last appearance of Dido in the poem Virgil has strengthened and deepened the pathos by reminiscences both from his own poem and from other epic poets. Throughout the *Aeneid* this technique is constantly used (indeed most Roman poets considered that the literature of the past offered a rich heritage on which they could build, a view which has been shared by many of the greatest English writers), and in this respect the passage gives a microcosmic illustration of Virgil's poetic method.

4. Analysis of 12.930–52

The final scene of the poem begins with the words 'Turnus, brought low ...'. There is no longer any question of the issue of the single combat: Aeneas has won. The phrase 'brought low' indicates that the violence and arrogance, the pride of Turnus has been extinguished: to tame the proud (*debellare superbos*, 6.853 – translated as 'firmness against aggressors') was part of the Roman mission, to be followed by sparing the conquered (*parcere subiectis*, 6.853 – translated as 'generosity to the conquered'). Thus in Turnus' case the taming of the proud has been achieved, and we now look for the sparing of the conquered.

The expectation of mercy is built up by the description of Turnus – 'a pleading hand', 'in appeal', and by his honourable speech admitting defeat and accepting that the loser can make no demands ('I know, I've deserved it'), and appealing for mercy in the name of his old father Daunus. This is an appeal especially likely to move Aeneas in view of his filial devotion to his old father Anchises, whom Turnus mentions. And Turnus' last words 'Don't carry hatred further' are precisely the sort of appeal to which Aeneas is bound to listen, as all through the poem he has fought a war which he did not want to fight, and wished to end as bloodlessly as possible.

At the end of Turnus' speech the action is held in suspense as Aeneas hesitates, and is clearly preparing to spare him until he sees the belt which Turnus had stripped from Pallas and was now wearing. Aeneas had been entrusted with responsibility for the young Pallas by his father Evander, and had travelled side by side with him on the way to the war. After the news of Pallas' death had been reported back to Evander, the unhappy father had only one request to make of Aeneas, that he should exact vengeance from Turnus (11.178f.). Turnus' behaviour in his triumph over Pallas had been arrogant and cruel (10.441 ff.), and when the news had come to Aeneas his reactions were wild and uncontrolled (10.510ff.). The description of Pallas' funeral at the beginning of Book 11 was presented with the deepest pathos. All these things are now recalled by Aeneas ('How well he knew it', 'a symbol of triumph and doom', 'this sad reminder of all the pain Pallas' death had caused'). The result is a loss of rational control ('Rage shook him. He looked frightening'); and it is in hot anger (950) and revenge (949) that Aeneas kills his suppliant.

These then were the reasons: the arrogance of Turnus in his victory over Pallas, Aeneas' grief, his obligations to Evander to exact vengeance. These reasons cause Aeneas to act in a way contrary to what we would expect of him, and contrary to the Roman ideal of mercy to the conquered. They are strong reasons (and we may think of Augustus' vengeance on the assassins of Julius Caesar as a parallel); but Virgil has certainly not suggested that they justify the act. Instead of ending the poem on a note of triumph for Aeneas' final achievement of his mission, he ends it not with the victor at all, but with the victim, as 'the unconsenting spirit fled to the shades below'.

Bibliography

The entries are listed in chronological order. For fuller information see *Greece and Rome, New Surveys in the Classics No. 1: Virgil* by R.D. Williams, 1967, reprinted with addenda, 1978.

Translations
Dryden (1697), Day Lewis (1952), Jackson Knight (prose, 1955), Copley (1965), Mandelbaum (1971), Fitzgerald (1984)

Literary criticism etc.

T.R. Glover, *Virgil* (London, 1904; seventh edn. 1942)

C. Bailey, *Religion in Virgil* (Oxford, 1935)

W.F. Jackson Knight, *Roman Vergil* (London, 1944; second edn. 1966)

C.M. Bowra, *From Virgil to Milton* (London, 1945)

T.S. Eliot, *What is a Classic?* (London, 1948)

V. Pöschl, *Die Dichtkunst Virgils: Bild und Symbol in der Aeneis* (Innsbruck, 1950, trans. Seligson, Michigan, 1962)

J. Perret, *Virgile, L'Homme et L'Oeuvre* (Paris, 1952; second edn. 1965)

Brooks Otis, *Virgil: a Study in Civilized Poetry* (Oxford, 1963)

A. Parry, *The Two Voices of Virgil's Aeneid* (*Arion* ii, 1963, pp. 66ff.)

M.C.J. Putnam, *The Poetry of the Aeneid* (Harvard, 1965)

Steele Commager (ed.), *Twentieth Century Views: Virgil* (New Jersey, 1966)

F. Klingner, *Virgil: Bucolica, Georgica, Aeneis* (Zürich, 1967)

R.D. Williams, *Virgil* (*Greece and Rome, New Surveys in the Classics No. 1.*, Oxford, 1967)

K. Quinn, *Virgil's Aeneid: a Critical Description* (London, 1968)

W.S. Anderson, *The Art of the Aeneid* (New Jersey, 1969)

D.R. Dudley (ed.), *Virgil (Studies in Latin Literature and its Influence*, London, 1969)

W.A. Camps, *An Introduction to Virgil's Aeneid* (Cambridge, 1969)

R.D. Williams, *Aeneas and the Roman Hero* (Macmillan, 1973)

R.D. Williams, *The Aeneid of Virgil*, 2 vols. (Macmillan, 1972-3)

W.R. Johnson, *Darkness Visible: a study of Vergil's Aeneid* (California, 1975)

R.D. Williams and T.S. Pattie, *Virgil: His Poetry through the Ages* (British Library, 1982)

R.D. Williams, *Virgil: the Aeneid*, in *Cambridge History of Classical Literature*, vol. 2, pp. 333-69 (Cambridge, 1982)

Gordon Williams, *Technique and Ideas in the Aeneid* (New Haven, 1983)

K.W. Gransden, *Virgil's Iliad* (Cambridge, 1984)

Glossary

In the glossary I have listed all the names that are of any importance; I have generally omitted the names of warriors or places mentioned only once or twice, except where some explanation is needed to elucidate the text. The glossary is not an index, and I have given only the first reference to names which occur frequently.

Acesta: a town in Sicily, called Segesta by the Romans. 5.718.
Acestes: a Trojan prince, settled in Sicily, 1.195.
Achaean: Greek. 2.462.
Achates: Aeneas' close companion, 1.120.
Achemenides: a Greek left behind in Sicily by Odysseus, 3.614.
Acheron: a river of the underworld, 6.107.
Achilles: the most prominent Greek warrior, 1.30.
Acoetes: squire of Evander and Pallas, 11.30.
Acrisius: an ancient king of Argos, father of Danae, 7.372.
Actium: a promontory in W. Greece, site of Augustus' victory over Antony and Cleopatra, 3.280.
Adrastus: an Argive king who fought against the Thebans, 6.480.
Aeacus: grandfather of Achilles, 6.839.
Aegaeon: a giant, also called Briareus, 10.565.
Aeneas: a Trojan prince, hero of the poem, 1.92.
Aeolus: (i) king of the winds, ruler of Aeolia, an island north of Sicily, 1.52; (ii) a Trojan warrior, 12.542.
Aesculapius: god of medicine, 7.769.
Aetna: volcano in Sicily (Etna), 3.554.
Aetolia: an area of Greece from which Diomedes came, 10.28.
Agamemnon: leader of the Greek forces against Troy, 1.284.
Agathyrsi: a Scythian people, 4.146.
Agenor: a Carthaginian ancestor, 1.338.
Agrippa: a leading minister of Augustus, 8.682.
Agylla: another name for Caere in Etruria, 7.652.
Ajax: son of Oileus, who raped Cassandra in Minerva's temple, 1.41.
Alba Longa: the second settlement of the Trojans in Italy, 1.7.

Albunea: a grove and fountain in Latium, 7.83.

Alcides: son of Alceus, often used of Hercules, Alceus' grandson. 8.219.

Aletes: a Trojan elder, 1.121.

Allecto: one of the Furies, 7.325.

Almo: son of Tyrrheus, 7.532.

Aloeus: father of the giants Otus and Ephialtes, 6.582.

Alpheus: a river in S. Greece, 3.694.

Amata: queen of Latium, 7.343.

Amathus: town in Cyprus where Venus had a famous seat of worship, 10.51.

Amazons: warrior maidens, 1.491.

Ammon: an African name for Jupiter, 4.198.

Amphitryon: the mortal father of Hercules (he was actually son of Jupiter), 8.103.

Amsanctus: a valley in central Italy, 7.565.

Amyclae: a town in Latium, 10.564.

Amycus: (i) a Trojan, 1.221; (ii) boxer king of the Bebrycians, 5.373.

Anchises: father of Aeneas, 1.618.

Ancus: the fourth king of Rome, 6.815.

Androgeos: (i) a Greek killed at Troy, 2.370; (ii) a Cretan killed by the Athenians, 6.20.

Andromache: wife of Hector, 2.455.

Anius: a king of Delos, 3.80.

Anna: Dido's sister, 4.9.

Antandros: a town near Troy, 3.5.

Antenor: a Trojan who founded Patavium, 1.242.

Antheus: a Trojan commander, 1.182.

Antony: the Roman general defeated (with Cleopatra) by Augustus, 8.686.

Anubis: an Egyptian dog-headed god, 8.698.

Apollo: Phoebus Apollo, guardian god of Troy, famous for his oracles, patron deity of Augustus, 2.121.

Apulia: an area of S. Italy, 11.678.

Arcadians: a people of S. Greece, some of whom were led by Evander to Pallanteum on the site of Rome, 8.51.

Ardea: home of Turnus, 7.412.

Arethusa: nymph of a fountain in Sicily, 3.696.

Argiletum: a district of Rome, 8.345.

Argive: Greek, 1.46.

Argos: (i) a town and district of Greece, sometimes used for Greece itself, 1.285; (ii) a one-time friend of Evander, 8.346.

Argus: a hundred-eyed monster, guardian of Io, 7.791.

Ariadne: daughter of King Minos, lover of Theseus, 6.28.

Arpi: a city in S. Italy, home of the Greek Diomedes from Aetolia, 10.28.

Arruns: an Etruscan who killed Camilla, 11.759.

Ascanius: young son of Aeneas, also called Iulus, 1.267.

Assaracus: a Trojan ancestor, 6.650.

Astyanax: son of Hector and Andromache, 2.457.

Athene: Pallas Athene (Roman Minerva), patron goddess of the Greeks, 1.39.

Athesis: a river in N. Italy near the Po, 9.680.

Athos: a mountain in N. Greece, 12.701.

Atii: a Roman family to which Augustus' mother belonged, 5.568.

Atlas: a giant, also the name of his mountain in N. Africa, 1.741.

Atreus: father of Agamemnon and Menelaus, 1.457.

Atrides: sons of Atreus, 2.500.

Atys: a young Trojan, 5.569.

Aufidus: a river in S.E. Italy, 11.405.

Augustus: first emperor of Rome, 6.792.

Aulis: a port in N. Greece from which the Greeks sailed against Troy, 4.425.

Aunus: a Ligurian warrior, 11.699.

Aurora: goddess of the dawn, mother of Memnon, 1.751.

Aurunci: an Italian people of Campania, 7.206.

Ausonia: a name for Italy, 3.385.

Automedon: charioteer of Achilles, 2.477.

Aventinus: an Italian warrior born on the Aventine, one of Rome's seven hills, 7.656.

Avernus: a lake near Naples with a legendary entrance to the underworld, sometimes used to mean the underworld itself, 3.442.

Bacchante: a frenzied worshipper of Bacchus, 3.125.

Bacchus: god of wine, 1.734.

Bactra: an area of the Far East, 8.687.

Barcaei: a N. African tribe, 4.43.

Bebrycians: people of the Far North-east, 5.373.

Bellona: a goddess of war, 8.703.

Belus: father of Dido, 1.621.

Berecynthos: a mountain near Troy, 9.619.

Bitias: (i) a Carthaginian, 1.738; (ii) a Trojan, 9.672.

Briareus: a giant with a hundred arms, 6.287.

Brutus: the first consul of Rome, 6.817.
Butes: (i) a famous boxer, 5.372; (ii) an aged Trojan, 9.647; (iii) a Trojan warrior, 11.690.
Buthrotum: a Greek city in Epirus, 3.293.

Cacus: a monster killed by Hercules, 8.195.
Caeculus: an Italian warrior, founder of Praeneste, 7.678.
Caeneus: the maiden Caenis who was changed by Neptune into a man, 6.448.
Caere: an important city in Etruria, 8.478.
Caesar (Augustus): first emperor of Rome, 1.286.
Caesar (Julius): victor over Pompey in the civil wars, assassinated in 44 B.C., 6.830.
Caieta: a port in N.W. Italy, called after Aeneas' nurse, 6.900.
Calchas: a Trojan priest, 2.100.
Calliope: Muse of epic poetry, 9.525.
Calydon: a town whose king angered Diana, who then sent a wild boar to ravage the land, 7.306.
Camilla: a warrior princess assisting Turnus, 7.803.
Camillus: a Roman general reputed to have expelled the Gauls from Rome after they had captured it in 390 B.C., 6.825.
Capitol: the most important of Rome's seven hills, 6.836.
Capreae: an island near Naples, modern Capri, 7.735.
Capys: (i) a Trojan, 1.183; (ii) a king of Alba Longa, 6.768.
Carmental gate: a gate of Rome called after the nymph Carmentis, Evander's mother, 8.338.
Carpathian sea: near Crete, 5.595.
Carthage: city of N. Africa ruled by Dido and beloved by Juno, 1.13.
Cassandra: daughter of Priam, gifted with prophecy but fated never to be believed, 2.246.
Catiline: conspirator against the Roman Republic, 8.668.
Catillus: an Italian warrior, twin of Coras, 7.672.
Cato (the Elder): Roman statesman (early second century B.C.) of stern traditional virtues, 6.841.
Cato (the Younger): Roman statesman (mid-first century B.C.), a Stoic, proverbial for incorruptibility, 8.670.
Cayster: a river in Asia Minor, 7.702.
Celaeno: a Harpy, 3.212.
Centaurs: fabulous creatures, part horse, part man, 6.286.
Ceraunia: mountains in N.W. Greece, 3.506.
Cerberus: watch-dog of the underworld, 6.417.
Ceres: goddess of corn, 1.178.

Chaonia: district of N.W. Greece, 3.292.

Chaos: a primordial deity, 4.510.

Charon: ferryman of the underworld, 6.299.

Charybdis: a whirlpool opposite Scylla, located in the Straits of Messina, 3.420.

Chimaera: a fabulous monster like a dragon, 6.288.

Circe: a witch, 3.386.

Cithaeron: a mountain in N. Greece, 4.303.

Clausus: an Italian warrior, ancestor of the Claudii, 7.706.

Cleopatra: queen of Egypt, ally of Antony against Augustus, 8.696.

Cloanthus: a Trojan, 1.222.

Cloelia: a Roman maiden who swam the Tiber to escape from captivity, 8.651.

Clusium: an Etruscan city, 10.168.

Cocles: Horatius Cocles who held the bridge against the invading troops under Lars Porsenna, 8.650.

Cocytus: a river of the underworld, 6.132.

Coeus: a Titan, son of Earth, 4.180.

Coras: founder of Tibur, an Italian warrior, 7.672.

Corcyra: an island off W. Greece, modern Corfu, 3.291.

Coroebus: a Trojan, lover of Cassandra, 2.341.

Corybantes: worshippers of the goddess Cybele, 3.111.

Corythus: a town in Etruria called after its founder, 3.170.

Cossus: a Roman warrior of the fifth century B.C., 6.841.

Creusa: Aeneas' Trojan wife, 2.562.

Cumae: town near Naples, site of Apollo's temple near the entrance to the underworld, 3.441.

Cupid: god of love, son of Venus, 1.658.

Cures: a small Sabine town, home-town of Numa, the second king of Rome, 6.811.

Cybele: the mother of the gods (*Magna Mater*), worshipped especially on Mt Berecynthus near Troy, 3.113.

Cyclades: islands in the Aegean sea, 3.126.

Cyclops: fabulous one-eyed giants, 1.201.

Cyllene: a mountain in Arcadia, 8.139.

Cymodoce: a sea-nymph, 10.225.

Cynthus: a mountain in Delos, 1.498.

Cythera: an island off S. Greece, reputed birthplace of Venus (hence called Cytherea), 1.257.

Daedalus: master craftsman of legend, 6.14.

Danae: legendary founder of Ardea, 7.410.

Danai: the Greeks, 3.288.

Dardan: Trojan, 2.786.

Dardanus: founder of Troy, 3.167.

Dares: a Trojan boxer, 5.368.

Daunus: father of Turnus, 10.616.

Decii: a Roman family, two of whom achieved fame by devoting themselves to death on the battlefield, 6.824.

Deiphobe: name of the Sibyl, 6.36.

Deiphobus: son of Priam, 2.310.

Delos: an island in the Aegean, sacred to Apollo, 3.124.

Diana: goddess of hunting, sister of Apollo, 1.499.

Dicte: a mountain in Crete, 4.72.

Dido: queen of Carthage, 1.299.

Dindymus: a mountain near Troy, 9.618.

Diomed (Diomedes): a famous Greek warrior, 1.96.

Diores: a son of Priam, 5.297.

Dis: ruler of the underworld (Pluto), 6.269.

Dodona: site of a famous shrine of Jupiter in N.W. Greece, 3.466.

Dolon: a Trojan warrior killed at Troy, 12.347.

Dolopes: Thessalian followers of Achilles, 2.29.

Donysa: an island in the Aegean, 3.125.

Drances: a Rutulian, opposed to Turnus, 11.122.

Drusi: a famous Roman family, very prominent in Augustus' time, 6.824.

Dryopes: a people of N. Greece, 4.145.

—

Egeria: a nymph, 7.763.

Electra: daughter of Atlas, mother of Dardanus, 8.135.

Elis: a district in S. Greece, 3.694.

Elissa: Dido's other name, 4.335.

Elysium: the place of the blessed in the underworld, 5.735.

Enceladus: a giant who rebelled against Jupiter, 3.578.

Entellus: a Sicilian boxer, 5.387.

Epeus: a Greek warrior, builder of the wooden horse, 2.264.

Epirus: a district in N.W. Greece, 3.292.

Erebus: a name for the underworld, 4.510.

Eridanus: the river Po, 6.659.

Eriphyle: wife of Amphiaraus, killed by her son, 6.446.

Erymanthus: a mountain in Arcadia, 5.449.

Eryx: (i) a Sicilian hero, half-brother of Aeneas, a famous boxer, 5.23; (ii) a mountain in Sicily, 5.759.

Etruria: a district north of Rome, whose inhabitants were called

Etruscans or Tuscans, 7.43.

Euboea: an island to the east of Greece, 6.2.

Eumedes: a Trojan, son of Dolon, 12.346.

Euphrates: a river in Mesopotamia, 8.726.

Eurotas: the river on which Sparta stood, 1.498.

Euryalus: a young Trojan warrior, 5.294.

Eurystheus: King of Mycenae at whose orders Hercules undertook his twelve labours, 8.293.

Eurytion: a Trojan, competitor in the archery contest, 5.495.

Evadne: wife of Capaneus who killed herself on his pyre, 6.447.

Evander: Arcadian king living at Pallanteum on the future site of Rome, ally of Aeneas, 8.52.

Fabii: a famous Roman family, including Quintus Fabius Maximus who saved the Romans in the war against Hannibal at their moment of extreme crisis, 6.845.

Fabricius: a Roman of the third century, renowned for his simple life, 6.843.

Faunus: a Latin king, father of Latinus, who became a rural deity, 7.47.

Gaetuli: an African people, 4.40.

Galaesus: a Latin shepherd, 7.535.

Ganymede: a young Trojan, beloved by Jupiter, 1.28.

Garamantes: an Eastern people, 6.795.

Geryon: a giant, 6.289.

Getae: a people of Thrace, 7.604.

Glaucus: (i) a sea-deity, 5.823; (ii) a Trojan warrior, 6.483.

Gnossian: Cretan, from Gnossos (Cnossos) the chief town in Crete, 5.307.

Gorgon: a monster of mythology, 2.616.

Gracchi: a Roman family, famous especially in the second century B.C., 6.842.

Gradivus: another name of Mars, 3.35.

Gyarus: an island near Delos in the Aegean, 3.76.

Gyas: a Trojan, 1.222.

Hades: the underworld, 2.398.

Halaesus: an Italian general, 7.723.

Harpalyce: a Thracian nymph, 1.316.

Harpies: supernatural monsters, 3.212.

Hebrus: a river in Thrace, 12.331.

Hecate: Diana as goddess of the underworld, possessed of sinister and magical powers, 4.511.

Hector: the chief Trojan warrior, 1.99.

Hecuba: queen of Troy, wife of Priam, 2.501.

Helen: wife of Menelaus of Sparta, carried off by Paris to Troy (this was the cause of the Trojan War), 1.650.

Helenor: a Trojan warrior, 9.544.

Helenus: a Trojan prophet, 3.295.

Helicon: mountain of the Muses (in N. Greece), 7.641.

Hercules: a mortal deified for his services to mankind in killing monsters, son of Amphitryon, grandson of Alceus, 3.551.

Hermione: daughter of Menelaus and Helen, 3.328.

Hermus: a river in Lydia, 7.721.

Hesione: daughter of Laomedon, 8.158.

Hesperia: Italy, 1.530.

Hesperides: keepers of the golden apples, 4.484.

Hippocoon: a Trojan competitor in the archery contest, 5.491.

Hippolyta: a queen of the Amazons, the warrior-maidens, 11.661.

Hippolytus: son of Theseus, beloved by his step-mother Phaedra, 7.761.

Homole: a mountain in Thessaly, 7.676.

Hydra: a fabulous monster, 6.287.

Hymen: god of marriage, 4.127.

Hyrcanians: a people near the Caspian Sea, 4.367.

Iapis: a Trojan doctor, 12.391.

Iarbas: an African suitor of Dido, 4.36.

Iasius: brother of Dardanus, 3.168.

Iberians: a Spanish race, 7.663.

Icarus: son of Daedalus, 6.31.

Ida: (i) a mountain near Troy, 2.697; (ii) a mountain in Crete, 3.105.

Idalium: a mountain in Cyprus, sacred to Venus, 1.681.

Idomeneus: a king of Crete, 3.121.

Ilia: also called Rhea Silvia, mother of Romulus and Remus, 6.779.

Ilioneus: a Trojan leader, 1.120.

Ilium: Troy, 1.98.

Illyria: an area on the N.E. coast of the Adriatic, 1.243.

Ilus: (i) a Trojan ancestor, 6.650; (ii) Ascanius, 1.268; (iii) a Rutulian warrior, 10.400.

Inachus: an early Argive king, also a river-god, 7.286.

Inarime: a volcanic island near Naples, 9.716.

Io: daughter of Inachus, persecuted by Juno, 7.790.
Ionian Sea: a sea to the west of Greece, 3.211.
Iopas: a minstrel, 1.740.
Iris: goddess of the rainbow, messenger of Juno, 4.694.
Italus: a legendary ancestor of the Italians, 7.178.
Ithaca: an island off W. Greece, home of Odysseus, 2.104.
Iulus: another name for Ascanius, Aeneas' son, 1.267.
Ixion: a Lapith who was punished in Tartarus for assaulting Juno, 6.601.

Janiculum: a hill in Rome, 8.358.
Janus: the two-faced god who looked both ways, 7.180.
Jove: see Jupiter.
Julius: a name of Augustus, 1.287.
Juno: queen of heaven hostile to the Trojans, 1.4.
Jupiter: (also Jove) king of the gods, 1.223.
Juturna: a river nymph, sister of Turnus, 12.138.

Lacaenian: Spartan, 6.511.
Laertes: father of Ulysses (Odysseus), 3.272.
Laocoon: a Trojan priest, 2.41.
Laodamia: wife of Protesilaus who chose to die when her husband was killed, 6.447.
Laomedon: an early Trojan king who cheated the gods, 3.247.
Lapiths: a people of Thessaly, 6.601.
Larissaean: an epithet of Achilles who came from Pthia near Larissa in Thessaly, 2.197.
Latins: the inhabitants of Latium, 5.598.
Latinus: king of the Laurentians and of all Latium, 6.891.
Latium: the area where Aeneas landed, adjoining the Tiber, 1.6.
Latona: mother of Apollo and Diana, 1.502.
Laurentians: the people of Latium, 5.797.
Laurentum: the capital city of King Latinus, 10.672.
Lausus: son of Mezentius, 7.649.
Lavinia: daughter of King Latinus, subsequently wife of Aeneas, 6.764.
Lavinium: the name of Aeneas' first settlement in Italy, called after Lavinia, 1.2.
Leda: mother of Helen by Jupiter, 1.652.
Lemnos: an island in the Aegean, special seat of Vulcan's worship, 8.454.
Lerna: a marsh in S. Greece where Hercules killed the Hydra, 6.287.

Lethe: the river of forgetfulness in the underworld, 5.855.

Leucata: a promontory on the island of Leucas, off W. Greece, 3.274.

Liburnians: a people of Illyria, 1.244.

Libya: a wide area of N.Africa including Dido's city of Carthage, 1.22.

Ligurians: a people of N. Italy, 10.186.

Limbo: the area in the underworld of the untimely dead, 6.478.

Lipare: a volcanic island, north of Sicily, 8.416.

Locri: a people of central Greece, some of whom settled in S. Italy, 3.399.

Lupercal: an area of Rome, 8.343.

Luperci: a college of Roman priests, 8.664.

Lycaean: an epithet of the god Pan, from Mt Lycaeus in Arcadia, 8.344.

Lycia: an area in Asia Minor, 1.113.

Lyctian: Cretan, from the town Lyctos, 3.400.

Lycus: a Trojan warrior, 1.221.

Lydia: an area in Asia Minor from which the Etruscans were said to have come, 2.781.

Maeonia: another name for Lydia, 10.141.

Maia: daughter of Atlas, mother of Mercury, 8.138.

Malea: the southernmost tip of Greece, 5.193.

Manlius: Roman general who defended the Capital against the Gauls, 8.652.

Mantua: Virgil's birthplace in N. Italy, 10.200.

Marcellus: (i) Roman general of the third century B.C., 6.855; (ii) his descendant, nephew of Augustus, 6.883.

Mars: god of war, father of Romulus, 1.274.

Marsian hills: an area of central Italy, 7.758.

Massic country: an area in Campania, 7.726.

Massylian: belonging to the area near Carthage, 4.132.

Megaera: a Fury, 12.847.

Meliboean: Thessalian, 3.402.

Memnon: an Aethiopian general, ally of the Trojans, 1.489.

Menelaus: son of Atreus, brother of Agamemnon, husband of Helen, 2.263.

Mercury: divine messenger of Jupiter (Greek Hermes), 1.297.

Messapus: a prominent Latin general, 7.691.

Metabus: father of Camilla, 11.539.

Metiscus: the charioteer of Turnus, 12.469.

Mettus: a treacherous Alban, 8.642.

Mezentius: an expelled Etruscan tyrant, 7.647.
Mincius: a river in N. Italy, flowing into Lake Benacus, 10.206.
Minerva: see Athene, 2.32.
Minos: a Cretan king, after his death a judge in the underworld, 6.14.
Minotaur: a fabulous monster, 6.26.
Misenus: a Trojan bugler, 3.239.
Mnestheus: a prominent Trojan general, 4.288.
Murranus: a Latin warrior, 12.529.
Musaeus: a legendary musician, 6.667.
Mycenae: capital of King Agamemnon, sometimes used for the whole of Greece, 1.651.
Myconos: an island near Delos in the Aegean, 3.76.
Myrmidons: the troops of Achilles, 2.7.

Narycian: an epithet of the Locri, from one of their towns, 3.399.
Nautes: a Trojan soothsayer, 5.704.
Naxos: an island in the Aegean, 3.125.
Nemea: a place in S. Greece where Hercules killed the lion, 8.295.
Neoptolemus: (also called Pyrrhus) son of Achilles, grandson of Peleus, 2.263.
Neptune: god of the sea (Greek Poseidon), 1.124.
Nereid: a sea-nymph, 1.144.
Nereus: a god of the sea, 2.418.
Nisus: a Trojan warrior, 5.294.
Numa: second king of Rome, 6.812.
Numanus: a Rutulian warrior, 9.592.
Numicius: a tributory of the Tiber, 7.151.
Numidians: an African tribe, 4.41.
Numitor: a king of Alba Longa, 6.768.
Nysa: a mountain in Asia Minor, 6.805.

Oebalus: an ally of Turnus, 7.733.
Oechalia: a town in Euboea, 8.291.
Oenotrians: early Italians, 1.532.
Olearos: an island in the Aegean, 3.126.
Olympus: a Thessalian mountain, the abode of the gods, 4.269.
Opis: a nymph, 11.533.
Orcus: the underworld, 4.243.
Oreads: mountain nymphs, 1.499.
Orestes: son of Agamemnon, husband of Hermione, 3.330.
Oricum: a place in N.W. Greece, 10.136.

Orion: a famous huntsman, also a constellation, 1.535.
Orontes: a Lycian ally of Aeneas, 1.113.
Orpheus: a legendary musician, 6.119.
Othrys: a mountain in Thessaly, 7.676.

Pachynum: the S.E. promontory of Sicily, 3.430.
Pactolus: the 'golden river' of Lydia, 10.142.
Padusa: a river of N. Italy, 11.457.
Palamedes: a Greek, 2.51.
Palici: Sicilian deities, 9.584.
Palinurus: the chief Trojan helmsman, 3.201.
Pallanteum: city of Evander, on the site of future Rome, 8.54.
Pallas: (i) see Athene; (ii) an Arcadian ancestor, 8.51; (iii) son of Evander, 8.104.
Pan: a Greek rural deity, 8.344.
Pandarus: (i) a Lycian archer, 5.496; (ii) a Trojan warrior, 9.672.
Panthus: a Trojan priest, 2.318.
Paphos: a seat of Venus' worship in Cyprus, 1.415.
Paris: the Trojan prince who carried off Helen, 1.27.
Paros: an island in the Aegean, 3.126.
Parthenopaeus: an Argive warrior, 6.480.
Parthians: a people on the eastern frontier of Rome's empire, famous for their archery, 7.606.
Pasiphae: wife of King Minos of Crete, mother of the Minotaur, 6.24.
Pelasgians: a name for the Greeks, 8.600.
Peleus: grandfather of Neoptolemus, father of Achilles, 2.263.
Pelorus: the N.E. tip of Sicily, 3.411.
Penthesilea: queen of the Amazon warrior-maidens, 1.490.
Pentheus: king of Thebes, driven demented by Bacchus, 4.469.
Pergamea: a city founded by Aeneas in Crete, called after Pergamum, 3.133.
Pergamum: the citadel of Troy, 3.350.
Petelia: a town in S. Italy, 3.401.
Phaedra: daughter of Minos who fell in love with her stepson Hippolytus, 6.445.
Phaethon: son of Helios, the sun god, 10.190.
Pheneus: a town in Arcadia, 8.165.
Philoctetes: a Greek warrior, 3.402.
Phineus: a Greek warrior, punished by the Harpies, 3.213.
Phlegethon: the burning river of the underworld, 6.265.
Phlegyas: a king of the Lapiths, 6.618.
Phoebus: see Apollo.

Phoenicians: a people on the E. coast of the Mediterranean, Dido's original home, 1.344.
Phorcus: a sea-deity, 5.240.
Phrygia: the area of Asia Minor in which Troy stood, 1.381.
Picus: an ancestor of Latinus, 7.48.
Pilumnus: an ancestor of Turnus, 9.4.
Pinarii: a Roman family associated with the worship of Hercules, 8.270.
Pirithous: a king of the Lapiths, friend of Theseus, 6.393.
Pluto: king of the underworld, also called Dis, 7.327.
Polites: a son of Priam, 2.526.
Pollux: twin of Castor, 6.120.
Polydorus: a son of Priam, 3.45.
Polyphemus: a Cyclops, 3.641.
Pompey: opponent of Julius Caesar in the civil wars, 6.831.
Porsenna: an Etruscan king, 8.646.
Portunus: a sea-god of harbours, 5.241.
Potitii: a Roman family connected with the worship of Hercules, 8.269.
Praeneste: a town in Latium, 7.678.
Priam: king of Troy, 1.461.
Privernum: a town in Latium, 11.539.
Procas: a king of Alba Longa, 6.767.
Prochyta: an island near Naples, 9.715.
Procris: wife of Cephalus, accidentally killed by him, 6.445.
Proserpine: queen of the underworld, 4.698.
Proteus: a sea-god who could transform himself into various shapes, 11.263.
Pygmalion: Dido's brother, 1.347.
Pyrrhus: son of Achilles, also called Neoptolemus, 2.469.

Quirinus: a Roman deity, sometimes identified with Romulus, 6.859.

Remus: (i) brother of Romulus, 1.292; (ii) a Rutulian warrior, 9.330.
Rhadamanthus: a judge in the underworld, 6.566.
Rhaebus: the horse of Mezentius, 10.861.
Rhamnes: a Rutulian prophet, 9.325.
Rhesus: a king of Thrace, ally of the Trojans, 1.470.
Rhipeus: a Trojan warrior killed at Troy, 2.339.
Rhoetean: a shore near Troy, 6.505.
Romulus: founder of Rome, 1.275.

Rutulians: the Italian people led by Turnus against Aeneas, 7.472.

Sabaean: Arabian, 1.417.
Sabines: a people near Rome, 7.609.
Sabinus: a legendary ancestor of the Sabines, 7.178.
Salamis: an island near Athens, 8.158.
Salii: a Roman college of priests, 8.285.
Salius: a competitor in the foot-race, 5.298.
Sallentines: a people of S. Italy, 3.401.
Salmoneus: a sinner punished in Tartarus, 6.585.
Samos: an island in the Aegean, 1.16.
Samothrace: an island in the Aegean, 7.208.
Sarpedon: an ally of the Trojans, killed at Troy, 1.100.
Saturn: king of heaven before Jupiter, associated with the Golden Age, 1.569.
Saturnian: a frequent epithet of Juno, daughter of Saturn, 5.606.
Scaean gate: the main gate of Troy, 2.612.
Scipio: (i) the conqueror of Carthage at Zama in 202 B.C.; (ii) the destroyer of Carthage in 146 B.C., 6.842.
Scylla: a monster with six necks who devoured sailors passing near her, 1.200.
Scyrian: of the isle of Scyros where Achilles' son Pyrrhus was born, 2.477.
Serestus: a Trojan leader, 1.611.
Sergestus: a Trojan leader, ancestor of the Sergian family, 1.510.
Serranus: (i) Regulus, a Roman general in the First Punic War, 6.844; (ii) a Rutulian, 9.335.
Sibyl: the prophetess of Apollo, 3.452.
Sidon: a Phoenician city, twin city of Tyre, from which Dido came to Carthage, 1.613.
Sigean: straits near Troy, 2.312.
Sila: a mountain range in S. Italy, 12.715.
Silvanus: a Roman rural deity, 8.602.
Silvia: daughter of the Italian Tyrrheus, 7.487.
Silvius: son of Aeneas and Lavinia, dynasty name of the Alban kings, 6.763.
Simois: one of the rivers of Troy, 1.100.
Sinon: a Greek who deceived the Trojans over the wooden horse, 2.79.
Sirens: fabulous maidens who charmed sailors to destruction by their song, 5.864.
Soracte: an Etruscan mountain, 7.696.

Sparta: a city in S. Greece, ruled by Menelaus, 1.316.
Strophades: islands off the W. coast of Greece, home of the Harpies, 3.209.
Strymon: a river in Thrace, 10.265.
Styx: a river of the underworld, 5.855.
Sychaeus: husband of Dido, murdered by Pygmalion, 1.343.
Symaethus: a river in Sicily, 9.584.
Syracuse: a famous city in E. Sicily, 3.693.
Syrtes: quicksands off Carthage, 1.111.

Taburnus: a mountain in central Italy, 12.715.
Tarchon: leader of the Etruscan contingent sent to aid Aeneas, 8.505.
Tarentum: an important town in S. Italy, 3.551.
Tarpeian heights: a cliff on the Capitol hill of Rome, 8.347.
Tarquin kings: the fifth king of Rome, Tarquinius Priscus, and the seventh and last, Tarquinius Superbus, 6.817.
Tartarus: the bottommost pit of Hell, sometimes used generally for Hell itself, 4.243.
Tatius: an early king of the Sabines, 8.638.
Tegea: a town in S. Greece, 5.299.
Teleboeans: a people from Greece who settled in Capri, 7.735.
Tenedos: an island near Troy, 2.21.
Teucer: (i) a Trojan ancestor, 3.107; (ii) a Greek of Salamis, 1.619.
Teucrians: Trojans, 2.747.
Thebes: (i) a town in central Greece, 4.470; (ii) a town in Asia Minor, 9.698.
Thermodon: a river near the Black Sea, 11.661.
Theseus: a king of ancient Athens, 6.30.
Thessalians: a people of N. Greece, 2.6.
Thetis: the mother of Achilles, 8.384.
Thrace: a remote area of N. Greece, 1.316.
Tiber: the river on which Pallanteum, and later Rome, stood, 1.13.
Tiberinus: god of the Tiber, 8.33.
Tibur: a town in Latium, 7.630.
Timavus: a river in Illyria, 1.244.
Tiryns: a town in S. Greece from which Hercules came, 7.662.
Tisiphone: one of the Furies, 6.555.
Titans: a race of giants who rebelled against Jupiter, 6.580.
Tithonus: the mortal husband of the dawn-goddess Aurora, 4.584.

Tityos: a rebellious giant, 6.595.

Tmarian: from Tmarus in N.W. Greece, 5.621.

Tolumnius: a Latin augur, 11.429.

Torquatus: a Roman warrior who put his son to death for having fought out of line, 6.824.

Trinacria: Sicily, 3.554.

Triton: a sea deity, 1.144.

Tritonian: an epithet of Athene from Lake Triton in N. Africa where she was said to have been born, 11.483.

Trivia: a name of Diana, as goddess of the cross-roads, 6.35.

Troilus: youngest son of Priam, 1.474.

Tullus: the third king of Rome, 6.815.

Turnus: leader of the Rutulians, 7.55.

Tuscan: of Etruria (Etruscan), the area north of the Tiber, 7.209.

Tydeus: father of Diomedes, famous in the Argive war against Thebes, 6.479.

Tyndareus: father of Helen, 2.569.

Typhoeus: a Titan, punished by being buried under a volcano, 8.298.

Tyre: sister-city of Sidon in Phoenicia, from which Dido came to Carthage, 1.12; hence Carthaginians are called Tyrians.

Tyrrhene: Etruscan, 1.67.

Tyrrheus: an Italian, father of Silvia, 7.485.

Ufens: an Italian general, 7.744.

Ulysses: a Greek general (Odysseus), especially hated by the Trojans for his trickery, 2.7.

Umbro: an Italian general, 7.752.

Velia: a port south of Naples where Palinurus was murdered, 6.366.

Venilia: a nymph, mother of Turnus, 10.76.

Venulus: an Italian ambassador to Diomedes, 8.9.

Venus: goddess of love, mother and protector of Aeneas, 1.227.

Vesta: goddess of the hearth, 2.296.

Vesulus: a mountain of N. Italy, 10.509.

Virbius: (i) Hippolytus, 7.777; (ii) a son of Hippolytus, 7.762.

Volcens: a Latin general, 9.370.

Volscians: a people of Latium, 7.803.

Vulcan: god of fire, husband of Venus, 7.680.

Xanthus: a river of Troy, 1.473.